Essential Aikido
An Illustrated Handbook

Other Aikido books by Nick Waites

Aikido and Kuzushi

ISBN 978-1-326-41575-4

Koteikan Press, 2016

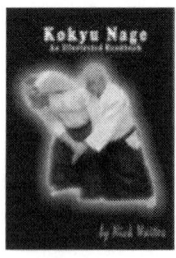

Kokyu Nage – An Illustrated Handbook

ISBN 978-1-326-22677-0

Koteikan Press, 2015

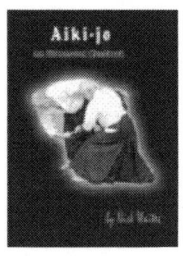

Aiki-jo – An Illustrated Handbook

ISBN 978-1-291-84466-5

Koteikan Press, 2014

Progressive Aikido – An Illustrated Handbook

ISBN 978-1-291-75107-9

Koteikan Press, 2014

Aikido Body, Mind and Spirit – The Further Teachings of Alex Essani

ISBN 978-0-95388-485-8

Koteikan Press, 2012

 Aikido, Iron Balls and Elbow Power – The Teachings of Alex Essani

ISBN 978-0-9538848-4-1

Koteikan Press, 2008

Essential Aikido
An Illustrated Handbook

Nick Waites

Kōteikan Press 2017

Copyright © 2021 by Nick Waites

All rights reserved. This book or any portion thereof may not be reproduced or used in any manner whatsoever without the express written permission of the publisher except for the use of brief quotations in a book review or scholarly journal.

First Printing: 2013

ISBN 9781549845239

Koteikan Press

www.aikido-koteikan.co.uk

CONTENTS

Acknowledgements xiii

Preface xiv

About Aikido xv

Morihei Ueshiba, the Founder of Aikido xvi

Japanese Aikido terms xvi

PART 1: BASICS 17

Dojo Etiquette 18

The Aikido uniform 20

Tying the obi (belt) 20

Aikido weapons 21

Jo 21

Bokken 21

Tanto 21

Posture 22

Tai-sabaki 22

Continuity of consciousness 22

Sequential movement 22

Ki contact 23

Relaxation 23

Extension 23

Timing 24

Kuzushi 24

Ukemi 25

Leading 26

Aikido attack forms 27

Grabs 27

Strikes	28
Rear attacks	29
PART 2: PREPARATORY EXERCISES	**31**
Seiza	**32**
Rei	**32**
Kamae	**33**
Kokyu	**34**
Breathing exercise #1	34
Breathing exercise #2	35
Breathing exercise #3	36
Junbi taiso	**37**
Arm swinging	37
Side stretch	38
Back bend	38
Back rotation	39
Leg stretch 1	39
Leg stretch 2	40
Hip Stretch	40
Wrist exercises	**41**
Nikyo #1	41
Nikyo #2	41
Sankyo	42
Kotegaeshi	42
Atemi	**43**
Shomen uchi	43
Yokomen uchi	43
Chudan tsuki	44

Jodan tsuki 44

Tori fune and Furitama 45

Tori fune 45

Furitama 45

Shikko 46

Suwari waza no Shikko 46

Ukemi 47

Mae ukemi 47

Ushiro ukemi 48

PART 3: TAI SABAKI 49

Kaiten: change direction 180° 50

Irimi-ashi: step forward 50

Yoko-ashi: step to the side 51

Okuri-ashi: step forward, front leg leading 51

Tenkan: full turn 52

Paired exercise 52

Han-tenkan: half/small turn 53

Sokumen: step to the side and turn 53

Paired exercise 53

Ushiro-sokumen: step back and turn 54

Paired exercise 54

Irimi-sokumen: diagonal step forward, side turn 55

Irimi-tenkan: step forward, full turn 56

Paired exercise 56

Irimi hantenkan: step diagonally forward, small turn 57

Paired exercise 57

Three attacks exercise 58

Part 4: Kihon Waza 60

Practice recommendations 61

Ikkyo 62

Kosa dori Ikkyo omote #1 63
Kosa dori Ikkyo ura #1 64
Shomen uchi Ikkyo omote #1 65
Shomen uchi Ikkyo ura #1 66
Jodan tsuki Ikkyo omote 67
Jodan tsuki Ikkyo ura 68
Katate dori Ikkyo omote #1 69
Katate dori Ikkyo ura #1 70
Chudan tsuki Ikkyo omote 71
Chudan tsuki Ikkyo ura 72
Kosa dori Ikkyo ura #2 73
Chudan tsuki Ikkyo ura #2 74

Nikyo 76

Kosa dori Nikyo omote 77
Kosa dori Nikyo ura 78
Shomen uchi Nikyo omote 79
Shomen uchi Nikyo ura 80
Katate dori Nikyo omote 81
Katate dori Nikyo ura 82
Yokomen uchi Nikyo omote 83
Yokomen uchi Nikyo ura 84

Sankyo 86

Kosa dori Sankyo omote 87
Kosa dori Sankyo ura 88

Shomen uchi Sankyo omote 89

Shomen uchi Sankyo ura 90

Jodan tsuki Sankyo omote 91

Jodan tsuki Sankyo ura 92

Katate dori Sankyo omote #1 93

Katate dori Sankyo ura #1 94

Yokomen uchi Sankyo omote 95

Yokomen uchi Sankyo ura 96

Katate dori Sankyo omote #2 97

Katate dori Sankyo ura #2 98

Chudan tsuki Sankyo omote 99

Irimi nage 100

Kosa dori Irimi nage #1 101

Shomen uchi Irimi nage #1 102

Kosa dori Iriminage #2 103

Shomen uchi Irimi nage #2 104

Katate dori irimi nage #1 105

Yokomen uchi irimi nage #1 106

Katate dori irimi nage #2 107

Yokomen uchi Irimi nage #2 108

Katate dori Irimi nage #3 109

Chudan tsuki Iriminage #1 110

Kosa dori Irimi nage #3 111

Chudan tsuki Irimi nage #2 112

Kosa dori Irimi nage #4 113

Jodan tsuki Irimi nage 114

Shiho nage 116

Kosa dori Shiho nage #1 117
Shomen uchi Shiho nage 118
Jodan tsuki Shiho nage 119
Katate dori Shiho nage #1 120
Yokomen uchi Shiho nage #1 121
Katate dori Shiho nage #2 122
Yokomen uchi Shiho nage #2 123
Katate dori Shiho nage #3 124
Chudan tsuki Shiho nage 125

Kote gaeshi 126

Kosa dori Kote gaeshi #1 127
Shomen uchi Kote gaeshi 128
Jodan tsuki Kote gaeshi 129
Katate dori Kote gaeshi #1 130
Yokomen uchi Kote gaeshi #1 131
Katate dori Kote gaeshi #2 132
Yokomen uchi Kote gaeshi #2 133
Kosa dori Kote gaeshi #2 134
Chudan tsuki Kote gaeshi 135

Kokyu nage 136

Kosa dori Kokyu nage #1 137
Shomen uchi Kokyu nage 138
Jodan tsuki Kokyu nage 139
Katate dori Kokyu nage #1 140
Yokomen uchi Kokyu nage #1 141
Katate dori Kokyu nage #2 142

Yokomen uchi Kokyu nage #2 143

Katate dori Kokyu nage #3 144

Chudan tsuki Kokyu nage #1 145

Glossary **146**

Acknowledgements

My special thanks go to Shaun Carr, Margaret Turner and Claire Byrne who patiently assisted me with photographic sessions and to Matthew Taylor for his photographic skills. I should also like to thank Margaret for her expert proof reading skills and John Goverts for his insights regarding the content of the book.

Preface

Aikido practice provides a wonderfully rich framework for personal exploration and development. However, for the beginner it involves a steep learning curve that may seem insurmountable. First there's the strict etiquette to observe, then there's the *Aikido* taxonomy in Japanese to learn, how to tie your *obi* (belt) correctly, how to sit, how to bow, how to fall down, how to stand up, how to attack... the list is never ending, and complex *Aikido* techniques have not yet been even mentioned. So it is not surprising that many beginners don't last beyond the first few weeks. Hence this book of essential information to make the transition from raw beginner to competent practitioner a little less daunting.

Everything that a beginner needs to know is contained in this book, explained and illustrated. But for experienced practitioners and instructors Parts 3 and 4, which cover *tai sabaki* (body movement) and *waza* (techniques) it also details a rational, systematic method for learning and teaching basic *Aikido* forms.

Your initial response to a physical attack is of utmost importance. You must instantly move to a position of relative safety and strategic advantage. In other words, you must move to the right place at the right time in order to avoid injury and simultaneously to be in a position to fully control the attacker. Once this is achieved you then have several options: whether to perform an *Aikido* technique to subdue or project your attacker away from you, strike a vulnerable point to disable the attacker, or simply move out of range of further aggression (running away will frequently be the most sensible choice, particularly if there are multiple attackers). This initial body movement (*tai-sabaki*) is one of the main topics explored in this book.

The training ideas described here involve the repeated practice of a small range of initial movements that can be applied to a large range of attack situations. These initial movements are mostly *katate-dori* based (*ai-hanmi* and *gyaku hanmi*) and they are all chosen to be directly applicable to the full range of strikes (*uchi*) that are normally practised in an *Aikido* dojo. In our experience, this consistency is not generally the case; rather, *katate-dori* techniques need to be adapted to strikes, sometimes quite radically. In the system described here no such adaptation is required. Consequently, fewer situations need to be considered. Moreover, each of these opening movements is exactly the same for many of the techniques that we typically practice.

There is good reason for the rich variety of *Aikido* techniques and their innumerable variations: by practising the full spectrum of *Aikido* techniques physical-mental-emotional coordination becomes highly tuned and the common principles at work emerge. However, practising a wide range of techniques can be bewildering and very daunting for a beginner. Many new starters give up very quickly because of this. So here we suggest a training system that provides a solid foundation of a relatively small number of key movements that are essential for further progress in the art. In our opinion, this approach is not only suitable for *Aikido* beginners but also as a method for internalising basic strategic principles for experienced practitioners. Bruce Lee is believed to have said that he would rather face an opponent who had practised many different kicks once than an opponent who had practised one single kick many times. The system we describe here is based on the same opinion: that it is better to practice a small range of exercises/techniques many times than a large range only briefly, so that each subject of study can be examined in depth.

About Aikido

The word 'ced*Aikido*' can be translated as 'Way of combining forces' or 'Way of harmony' or 'Way of harmony with ki', each translation confirming that *Aikido* is a non-aggressive martial art. The Founder of *Aikido*, the late Morihei Ueshiba, created *Aikido* as a means of dealing with aggressive intent without using unnecessary force, inflicting minimal injury to attackers by carefully subduing and controlling them.

The term 'aiki' refers to the principle of blending with an attacker's movements for the purpose of controlling their actions with minimal effort. An *Aikido* practitioner applies this principle by using the energy of the attacker to effect a counter-technique. The Founder said,

> '*In Aikido, we never attack. An attack is proof that one is out of control. Never run away from any kind of challenge, but do not try to suppress or control an opponent unnaturally. Let attackers come any way they like and then blend with them.*'

Aikido techniques therefore are directed at blending with and redirecting attacks rather than directly opposing them. This takes great skill, and perhaps this is one of the attractions of the art - that it is a study in mental and physical perfection. And when performed by expert practitioners, *Aikido* is gracefully dynamic and profoundly effective.

Sustained *Aikido* practice develops physical coordination and fitness, relaxed mind and body, self-awareness, self-confidence and general well-being. Time devoted to *Aikido* practice is never wasted, and the benefits it bestows on serious practitioners are very often profoundly life-changing.

Morihei Ueshiba, the Founder of Aikido

Morihei Ueshiba, (December 14, 1883 – April 26, 1969) was a famous martial artist and founder of the Japanese martial art of Aikido. He is often referred to as Kaiso, "the founder", or Ōsensei, "Great Teacher".

As a boy, he saw local thugs beat up his father for political reasons. He set out to make himself strong so that he could take revenge. He devoted himself to hard physical conditioning and eventually to the practice of martial arts, receiving certificates of mastery in several styles of jujitsu, fencing, and spear fighting. In spite of his impressive physical and martial capabilities, however, he felt very dissatisfied. He began delving into religions hoping to find a deeper significance to life, all the while continuing to pursue his studies of *budo* - the martial arts. By combining his martial training with his religious and political ideologies, he created the modern martial art of *Aikido*. Ueshiba decided on the name "aikido" in 1942 (before that he called his martial art "*aikibudo*" and "*aikinomichi*").

Ueshiba set up the Aikikai Hombu Dojo, Tokyo, in 1926. In the aftermath of the Second World War the *dojo* was closed, but Ueshiba continued training at another *dojo* he had set up in Iwama. From the end of the war until the 1960s, he worked to promote *Aikido* throughout Japan and abroad. He died from liver cancer in 1969. The Hombu Dojo is now the world headquarters of the Aikikai Foundation, the current head of which is the grandson of Morihei Ueshiba, Moriteru Ueshiba. He is referred to as 'Doshu'.

Though the underlying principles of *Aikido* remained unchanged, elements of the application, style and teaching varied over the decades for which Ueshiba taught. As a result, there are many different approaches to the practice of *Aikido* today. Some of Ueshiba's senior students founded their own schools of *Aikido*: Yoshinkan, founded by Gozo Shioda, Ki Aikido, by Koichi Tohei, and Shodokan, by Kenji Tomiki.

Japanese Aikido terms

The Japanese terms used throughout this book are shown in italics and are listed in the Glossary, along with an approximate pronunciation guide.

Part 1: Basics

This part of the book introduces basic information, especially useful for new starters in *Aikido*.

The sections on continuity of consciousness, sequential movement, and so on, have been included as introductions to concepts that really only become understandable with sustained practice. We realise that speaking about ki contact, extension, leading etc. could be meaningless, confusing or even off-putting for a complete beginner, but your awareness that these things exist is essential, otherwise practice can become just a mechanical process of technique assimilation, devoid of the important ingredients that make Aikido such a rich source of personal discovery and development.

As your *Aikido* evolves, and you no longer need to concentrate exclusively on how to move, where to move to, how to intercept attacks, and so on, only then will these apparently abstract concepts start to become clear and you will understand their importance to becoming an effective *Aikido* practitioner. But until that time, try to be patient and just practice.

Dojo Etiquette

Proper observance of etiquette is as much a part of our training as learning techniques.

It requires us to be constantly mindful, aware of our own actions and those of others. Etiquette teaches us to focus on details, such as how to sit, how to stand and how to be properly respectful to our teachers and our practice partners. Learning a martial art is full of such small details.

Each detail needs to be performed with sharp mental focus. For example, the etiquette involved in the simple act of stepping onto the *dojo tatami* (mat) can be used as an exercise in total awareness. You approach the edge of the mat, turn your back to it and step backwards onto the mat out of your *zori*, making sure that they are neatly placed and together. You sit in *seiza* and bow to the *dojo kamiza* (front of the *dojo* where a picture of the Founder is usually displayed) in the prescribed manner. Each step of the procedure should be performed with your attention directed to executing these simple actions perfectly. At the same time, you must be aware of the people nearby and be ready, for instance, to move quickly if there is the possibility of a collision with someone else on the mat.

Similarly, when we bow to a practice partner we should not do so casually. Each time it must be with real focus, our attention directed to the meaning of the gesture. To do otherwise is both disrespectful and insulting to our partners (who may notice our lack of etiquette if they are themselves properly focused!) Every instant of a training session should be utilised fully. These small, apparently insignificant, details all contribute to the development of sound *Aikido* skills. Furthermore, their development spills over into daily life where attention to detail is equally important to that in the *dojo*.

Aikido techniques can also be seen as collections of small details. We learn these details one by one with the aim, eventually, of integrating them into an uninterrupted stream of effective movements. The perfection of each detail is directly related to the perfection of the complete technique.

Standards of etiquette may vary somewhat from one *dojo* or organization to another, but the following guidelines are nearly universal. Please take matters of etiquette seriously.

- When entering or leaving the *dojo*, it is proper to bow in the direction of *O-sensei*'s (Morihei Ueshiba) picture, the *kamiza*, or the front of the *dojo*. You should also bow when stepping on to or leaving the mat.
- No shoes on the mat.
- Be on time for class. Students should be lined up and seated in *seiza* approximately 3-5 minutes before the official start of class. If you do happen to arrive late wait until the instructor grants permission to come on to the mat and join practice.
- If you should have to leave the mat or *dojo* for any reason during class, approach the instructor and ask permission.
- Avoid sitting on the mat with your back to the picture of *O-sensei*. Also, do not lean against the walls or sit with your legs stretched out. (Sit in *seiza* or, if you have a physical problem that prevents you from doing so, ask permission to sit cross-legged).
- Please keep talking during class to a minimum. What conversation there is should be restricted to one topic – Aikido. It is particularly impolite to talk while the instructor is addressing the class.
- Do not bring food, gum, or beverages onto the mat. It is also considered disrespectful in some *dojos* to bring open food or beverages into the *dojo*.
- Please keep your fingernails (and especially toenails) clean and cut short.
- Remove watches, rings and other jewellery before practice as they may catch your partner's hair, skin, or clothing and cause injury to oneself or one's partner.
- Do not engage in rough-housing or needless contests of strength during class.
- Change your clothes only in designated areas (not on the mat!).
- Remember that you are in class to learn, and not to gratify your ego. An attitude of receptivity and humility (though not obsequiousness) is therefore advised.

- Keep your training uniform clean, in good shape, and free of offensive odours.
- Your finger and toe nails should be short to avoid accidentally scratching practice partners.
- You probably will be expected to practice in bare feet so make sure that they are clean.
- Wear loose clothing if you don't have a *Karate* or *Judo* suit. Most *Aikido* people wear *Judo* suits for training.
- If you are having trouble with a technique, do not shout across the room to the instructor for help. First, try to figure out the technique by watching others. Effective observation is a skill you should strive to develop as well as any other in your training. If you still have trouble, approach the instructor at a convenient moment and ask for help.
- Carry out the directives of the instructor promptly. Do not keep the rest of the class waiting for you!
- It is usually considered polite to bow and say 'Thank you, *sensei*' upon receiving assistance or correction from the instructor. By all means ask for clarification if you don't quite understand your instructor's guidance, but do not try to make excuses for your imperfect performance.
- During class, if the instructor is assisting a group in your vicinity, it is frequently considered appropriate to suspend your own training and sit in *seiza* so that the instructor has adequate room to demonstrate.
- At the start and end of a class students sit in approximate order of rank and experience. The most senior students sit on the right of the mat (facing the *kamiza*) and the least experienced on the left.
- You will be expected to bow to a picture of the founder of *Aikido* at the start and end of classes. This has no religious significance – it is a Japanese tradition to show respect to the late Morihei Uyeshiba.
- You will also bow to your practice partners before and after practising with them.
- At the start of a class and also just before you begin training with a practice partner you should say "*Onegaeshimasu*" (pronounced Onny Gaishee Mass) and at the end of the class you will say "Thank you" formally in Japanese to your instructor: *Arigato Gozai Mashita* or *Domo Arigato Gozai Mashita* (Doe-moe Arree-gatto Gozai Mashta)
- Please pay your membership dues promptly. If, for any reason, you are unable to pay your dues on time, talk with the person in charge of dues collection. Sometimes special rates are available for those experiencing financial hardship.

The Aikido uniform

The white suit worn by *aikidoka* (practitioners of *Aikido*) is called a *keikogi* or just *gi* (practice clothing). It is usually a loose, plain white *judo* or *karate* suit. It is not usual for men to wear a tee shirt underneath the *keikogi* but for women it is usually required. Note that the jacket should always be tied with the left side over the right.

Most dojos require that *keikogi obi* (belt) is white unless you are *yudansha* (black belt). Some associations allow coloured belts according to grade. Your clothing should always be clean and odourless.

The traditional straw slippers worn in the *dojo* are called *zori*, but sandals such as flip-flops are acceptable substitutes.

The black or dark blue wide trousers, the *hakama*, traditionally worn by *aikidoka*, is usually reserved for *yudansha*, although women of a lower grade are also permitted to wear them. These rules vary with association so it is best to find out first before you begin to practice.

Tying the obi (belt)

There are several different methods of tying a martial arts belt. The knot shown below is probably the most commonly used in *Aikido*.

1) Find the mid-point of the belt and place it just below your navel.

2) Wrap it around your waist.

3) Cross the end in your right hand over the other end.

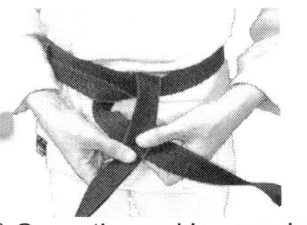

6) Cross the end in your right hand under the other end.

5) Pull the belt tight and bring your hands in front.

4) Tuck the end now in your left hand under both loops.

7) Thread the end now in your left hand through the opening between the ends.

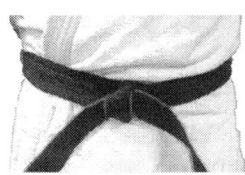

8) Pull the belt tight.

Aikido weapons

Three types of weapons are commonly used in *Aikido* training, namely

- *Jo* – wooden staff
- *Bokken* – wooden sword
- *Tanto* – wooden knife

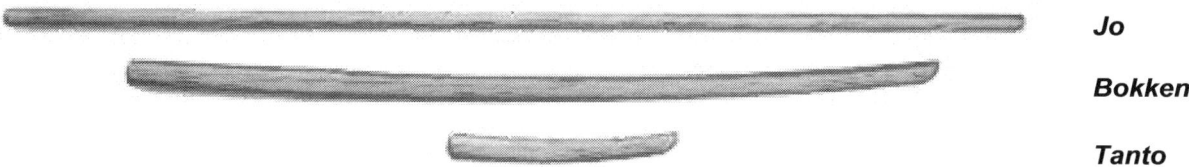

Jo

Bokken

Tanto

Jo

The *Aikido jo* is about 4.2 feet (1.3 metres) long and made from some form of hardwood, such as Oak. It is used in training as a weapon in its own right or as a training aid for unarmed *Aikido* practice. Forms of training with the *jo* include

1. *Jo suburi* – attack and defence forms practised solo
2. *Kumi jo* - attack and defence forms practiced with a partner
3. *Jo kata* – sequences of *jo* attack and defence forms practised solo
4. *Jo waza* – partner practice in which *tori* (the technique performer) holds the *jo* and *uke* (the attacker) grabs it with one or both hands. *Tori* applies *Aikido* techniques adapted to holding a *jo*.
5. *Jo dori* – *uke* (the attacker) attempts to strike *tori* (the defender) with the *jo*. *Tori* applies *Aikido* techniques adapted to attacks with a *jo*.

Bokken

The *bokken* is about 3.4 feet (1 metre) long and usually curved like a real Japanese sword (*katana*). It can be made from a variety of hardwoods, particularly those that are resistant to shock, such as Japanese Red and White Oak and Hickory. Like the *jo*, the *bokken* is used as a weapon in its own right and as a training aid for unarmed practice. Forms of training with the *bokken* include

1. *Bokken suburi* - attack and defence forms practised solo
2. *Kumi tachi* - basic attack and defence forms practised with a partner
3. *Bokken dori* – taking the *bokken* from an attacker.
4. *Bokken awase* – movement blending forms practised with a partner

Tanto

A typical *tanto* is usually between 1 - 1.25 feet (30-38 cm) long and made from some form of hardwood. It is generally only used as an aid to learning methods of disarming an attacker armed with a knife.

Posture

A good posture is the foundation upon which good *Aikido* technique is based. The basic *Aikido* posture is to stand with the front leg bent at the knee and the back leg straight, with most of the weight on the front leg. The front foot points directly forward or is turned slightly out. The rear foot is placed such that the arch of the foot is in line with the heel of the front foot. The back and neck form an approximately straight line with the rear leg. Arms are held in front of the body, hands open, fingers extended, ready to intercept an attack.

The gaze is not focused on any particular point in front even though you are facing forward. Rather, using peripheral vision, you expand your awareness as broadly as possible, trying to register everything and everyone within visual range.

Good posture gives the body stability, providing a solid basis for technique. Not only does a good posture look right, but it also provides a strong foundation for fast, controlled and effective movement. Without good posture, the body becomes easily unbalanced and lacks integration.

Use self–observation to check your posture at every opportunity until it becomes natural, not requiring any special effort of will to maintain. Experience and skill in *Aikido* are immediately apparent by observing the quality of a practitioner's posture.

Migi hanmi (right posture)

Tai-sabaki

Literally meaning 'body movement', *tai-sabaki* takes you to a strategically strong position as you respond to an attack and it is also an important component in the execution of a technique following from the initial response. Being in the right place at the right time is essential to the success of *Aikido* techniques, but more than that *tai-sabaki* keeps you out of danger from possible further attacks as you respond to *uke's* actions. Throughout the execution of a technique you must be in a defensively superior position to that of *uke*, and well-executed *tai-sabaki* ensures this. Various important forms of *tai-sabaki* are thoroughly explored in this book.

Continuity of consciousness

Being continuously aware of your physical state and that of your *uke* allows you to seamlessly modify your actions in response to his. For example, if *uke* blocks your attempt at performing a technique, rather than trying to force its execution you should immediately use the opposing force he is exerting to change to an appropriate alternative technique. This ability to adapt quickly to changing circumstances is only possible if you have a continuity of consciousness. Practising slowly and with full attention to the interaction between you and your partners will help you to develop this important ability.

Sequential movement

Body movement should be initiated from the *hara* (centre) and not from the arms and shoulders. The rule, 'body first, then arms' should be your guide for all body manoeuvres. You move your body towards the appropriate position momentarily before any arm movement occurs. In making a *tenkan* turn, for example, you move your body forward slightly before swinging your arm and turning to *uke's* side.

This principle of sequential movement is also a basic component of the *tori fune* exercise described later in Part 2.

Ki contact

Imagine gently pressing two spherical balloons together. Each balloon receives the same centre to centre force from the other and there exists a balance of forces. If one of the balloons is rotated slightly, this balance of forces is disturbed and they will spin away from each other. It takes only a tiny amount of effort to disturb the balloons' equilibrium no matter how forcefully, or gently, they are pressed together.

This example is analogous to the situation when *uke* and *tori* make physical contact with each other. For example, if *uke* grasps *tori*'s wrist there should be a feeling of two forces gently pressing towards each other, the direction of the mutual forces being directed towards each of the partners' centres. At the instant of contact the two opposing forces are in equilibrium, and this represents *ki* contact, the meeting of physical and mental energy. In this instance, *ki* contact is positive, the two energy fields being directed towards each other. *Uke*'s attacking *ki* is met by *tori*'s defensive *ki*, momentarily forming a light balance of forces. A defensive technique is initiated when *tori* disturbs the balance of forces by deflecting *uke*'s energy. In some instances, the attacking force may be so strong that the defensive force need only be minimal to disturb the balance. In other cases, the defensive force may need to be greater in order to supply the required level of *ki* contact. For example, if *uke* is energetically pushing *tori* away, he is providing most of the *ki* contact required and *tori* need only supply a little; on the other hand, *uke* may be pulling *tori* towards him, requiring *tori* to advance and supply enough *ki* contact to enable a technique to be performed. *Ki* contact should always be light but constant, neither too strong nor too weak.

When grabbed, our instinct is often to pull away from the direction of the grab. This represents negative *ki* contact and it generally impedes the application of technique. In *Judo* there is a saying, "When pulled, push; when pushed, pull." The *Aikido* equivalent could be "When pulled or pushed maintain the same constant *ki* contact." When you establish correct *ki* contact with an attacker, you provoke a physical and mental reaction; this *ki* provocation causes your attacker's energy to flow out towards you allowing you to join with it and redirect it.

Relaxation

Holding unnecessary tension in your body, particularly in your wrists, arms and shoulders, actually helps *uke* to control you. Tension gives *uke* too much information about your intention, allowing him to respond obstructively to your movements. Wrists, arms and shoulders should be in a relaxed but non-collapsible state, allowing full transmission of your energy through the point of contact (your wrist if that is where you are being held by *uke*). If you are in a state of optimal relaxation, *uke* will have nothing specific over which to exert control or offer resistance.

Moving from your *hara*, that is, your hip area, will naturally set your whole body state to that of calm relaxation, allowing you to move freely and efficiently.

Extension

This is a combination of aligning your body so that your defensive movement is as efficient as possible and directing your mental intention beyond the point of contact as you move. When *uke* grabs your wrist, your mental focus is likely to be directed to that point; you must move your mind well beyond that point so that you move through it rather than attempting to change its position by, for example, lifting your arm or forcing it to one side or the other. It is sometimes helpful to imagine that the index finger of your held wrist is directing a light beam onto whatever it is pointing at and continues to do so as you perform the technique. This directs your mental focus beyond your wrist and facilitates efficient transmission of your energy.

Timing

You must also ensure that you do not move too soon or too late. If you move too soon when, for example, you are attacked with *yokomen uchi*, your attacker will be able to follow your movement and perhaps overcome your defence. Moving too late, you will receive the full force of the attack. Your movement must be timed to make your attacker mistakenly feel that his attack will be successful.

Kuzushi

The Japanese word *kuzushi* literally means 'undermining' and in the context of martial arts it means destabilising and subsequently unbalancing an attacker as a precursor to the execution of a technique, whether a throw or immobilisation.

Continuous awareness of available *kuzushi* states during the execution of a technique allows it to be modified dynamically so that it concludes successfully. Moreover, consciously utilising *kuzushi* at technique inception can increase its effectiveness significantly. If *kuzushi* is ignored or imperfectly implemented, *tori* may need to use superior strength to unbalance and then control *uke*. Precise use of *kuzushi* enables *tori* to use minimal force to execute effective technique. Furthermore, the more complex the technique, the more likely it is that *uke* will be able to regain balance and oppose its completion, and therefore establishing and maintaining *kuzushi* throughout the duration of the technique's execution is essential.

The initial contact between *tori* and *uke* is of paramount importance. Establishing *uke's* instability as soon as there is physical contact determines technique efficacy. An attacker who is still on balance and stable following his initial attack is still highly dangerous. *Tori* must immediately destabilise *uke* prior to executing a technique. Failure to do so leaves *uke* with the potential to continue his attack.

Essential to the successful execution of *Aikido* techniques, *kuzushi* states neutralise attacking energy by destabilising the attacker on first contact. With accurate timing and control, *tori* can neutralise *uke's* attack using minimal force.

Identifying *kuzushi* states that occur during the execution of *Aikido* techniques serves to explain the underlying principles that make them effective. Consequently, *Aikido* practice is given an explicit, systematic modus operandi for the performance of effective technique. Moreover, where different styles of *Aikido* techniques appear to conflict with each other in terms of how basic principles are implemented, identifying the underlying *kuzushi* states can often explain why such technique variations can be equally effective.

Ukemi

Ukemi, the manner in which an *Aikido* technique is received, has two major purposes. The first is self-preservation. *Uke*, the attacker, provokes a defensive response from *tori*, the defender; this reversal of the roles of attacker and defender means that the attacker now needs to protect himself from any injury resulting from being thrown.

The second main purpose of *ukemi* is to learn how to become responsive to your partners' actions. There should be no real difference between the physical state in which you deliver an *Aikido* technique and the way in which you receive it. If there is a difference, it means that the *Aikido* principles of relaxation, contact and continuity of consciousness are lacking to some degree. A very good indicator of *Aikido* ability is the quality of the practitioner's *ukemi*.

For beginners, *ukemi* is simply learning how and when to fall in response to the delivery of an *Aikido* technique. This skill needs to become instinctive so that at more advanced levels of training, both attacks and defensive manoeuvres can be executed without reservation and without injury. However, in the beginning, *Aikido* practice partners need to help each other to allow development; it serves no constructive purpose for an experienced person to repeatedly block a beginner's technique unless it is for the purpose of highlighting a problem that subsequently will be corrected. Usually, however, it is best left to the instructor to identify and correct problems; students, irrespective of their experience, should simply practise together as harmoniously as possible.

At its best, *ukemi* is the ability to attack with full commitment, have continuity of consciousness throughout the execution of the technique, and at the same time be able to identify – although not necessarily exercise – opportunities for applying counter techniques. To *tori*, good *ukemi* feels like throwing air: *uke* attacks with full commitment, yet as soon as the initial attack has been neutralised, reacts by becoming acutely responsive to *tori*'s movements, neither holding back and resisting nor anticipating *tori*'s actions.

Moreover, *uke* should not become passive after the initial attack has been neutralised; a technique terminates only with a pin or a throw, so up to that point both participants, not just *tori*, should actively be involved in performing the technique. When taking *ukemi* you should feel that you are drawn to *tori* as if he were a magnet. *Tori's* task is to respond to your attack, using it to aid its neutralisation; *tori* has no need to drag you to an advantageous position simply to complete a technique if you are content to remain in a vulnerable position. As *uke* you must attempt to continue your attack as long as possible, at the same time trying to avoid placing yourself in a position that is strategically weak. Our practice does not generally require us to punish mistakes by striking our partners if they leave themselves vulnerable. However, both *tori* and *uke* should constantly look for such occurrences and try to find ways of avoiding them.

When your *ukemi* becomes highly responsive, *tori* must work much harder to perform technique, so his response to your attack is forced to improve; this encourages you to further refine your *ukemi* forcing *tori* also to further improve his technique. This mutual form of positive feedback leads to an upward spiral of improvement for both *uke* and *tori*.

When taking *ukemi* you should try to be light and responsive to the best of your ability, no matter what your opinion of the level of your partners' abilities. Uncooperative *ukemi*, that which 'tests' technique, teaches an experienced *tori* valuable lessons but teaches *uke* nothing. Finding ways to deal with such difficult partners is a good way for *tori* to learn about important concepts such as yielding, relaxation and balance. However, obstructive *ukemi* should only be practised when the class instructor requires it or your partner specifically requests it. Otherwise you should selfishly work on improving the quality of your own *ukemi*.

Ukemi is a skill that should progress in parallel with the ability to execute techniques. A good *uke* is not only rarely injured but is also so sensitive to partners' unintentionally imperfect actions that he could counter them easily. Moreover, practising with a gifted *uke* is an exhilarating experience.

Leading

Leading is the act of influencing your partner's attack by, for example, starting your defensive response before your partner actually touches you. For instance, if your partner reaches for your wrist and you wait until she grabs it before you start your defence, you will have to deal with her whole body hanging on to your arm. If, instead, you start the technique before she actually grabs you, you will be able to lead her attack to a place of your choosing, not hers. If you are already moving, and your partner is really committed to grabbing you, she will have to follow your movements, enabling you to lead her attack into any convenient *Aikido* form by just staying slightly ahead of her grab. All these aspects are interrelated; therefore, the ability to lead is dependent on both the timing previously mentioned and your partner's ability to perform *ukemi* well.

Leading allows you to influence how your partner will attack. For instance, you can provide your partner with a clear opening for her attack by extending a hand. Your hand then becomes either a much more tempting target or an obstacle that must be removed before her attack can succeed. By making it easy for your partner to attack you in a certain way, you are actually influencing her to attack you the way you want. In other words, you'll know ahead of time how you will be attacked, because you are giving her an opening too good to refuse. This is a great advantage to you - it removes your partner's element of surprise in the attack. Moreover, when your timing is right it works on a subconscious level, your attacker having no opportunity to be consciously aware that you are manipulating her.

Clearly then, timing is critical in leading your partner. If you lead too early, you will have moved before she has committed himself to an attack and she can simply abandon it and start again or quickly change to a different one; if you wait too long, you lose the advantage of leading.

Aikido attack forms

Aikido classes invariably involve partner practice in which *uke* (the attacker) attempts to grab or strike *tori* (the performer of the technique). The various forms of attack are illustrated below although in this book we deal with a smaller range of basic attacks (those that are highlighted).

Grabs

Kosa dori (Ai-hanmi katate dori)   Katate dori (Gyaku hanmi)

Ryote dori

Morote dori

Kata dori

Ryokata dori

Mune dori

Strikes

Shomen uchi | Yokomen uchi | Chudan tsuki

Jodan tsuki

Kata dori yokomen uchi

Kata dori jodan tsuki

Kata dori Shomen uchi (Kata menuchi)

Rear attacks

Ushiro ryote dori Ushiro mune dakeshime Ushiro katate dori kubishime

Ushiro eri dori Ushiro ryokata dori

Part 2: Preparatory Exercises

This part focuses on exercises that usually precede technique training. The exercises form a psycho-physical preparation for the main focus of a training session, relaxing body and mind while warming muscles and joints.

Preparatory exercise

Seiza

Seiza is the basic sitting posture adopted at the start and end of the class and during the class while the instructor is demonstrating.

Sit with your big toes just touching and your buttocks resting on your heels. Your back should be vertical. Your hands rest on your thighs and your arms and shoulders are relaxed. Look straight ahead.

Rei

At the beginning and end of a class there is a formal bow to the *Kamiza* (otherwise known as *Shomen*) where traditionally there is a photograph of Morihei Ueshiba, the founder of *Aikido*.

1) Sit in *seiza*.

2) 2) Keeping your back straight and head facing forward put your left hand palm down in front of you.

3) Your right hand follows so that your thumbs and index fingers form a triangle.

4) Bend forward at the waist keeping your buttocks touching your heels and your back as straight as possible.

6) Move right hand back to thigh and return to *seiza*.

5) L ift up your head until your arms are straight.

Kamae

In *Aikido,* ready posture is with the legs a comfortable distance apart, the feet one directly behind the other, the heel of the leading foot in line with the instep of the rear foot. The front knee is bent so that it is over the toes and the rear leg is straight. The shoulders are relaxed. The hands are raised to about waist height, fingers extended. The back is straight and the gaze is forward. The illustration shows *migi hanmi* (right posture). Left posture is *hidari hanmi*.

Migi hanmi (right posture)

Kokyu

Kokyu, or breathing exercises, calm the mind and promote mind-body coordination. Many such exercises exist but here we describe three that provide a good basis for practice. It is important to practice these exercises mindfully and slowly, paying attention to all details.

Breathing exercise #1

This breathing exercise involves moving the arms rhythmically to the side and to the front, at the same time coordinating the breathing and focusing the mind.

1) Stand with the feet about shoulder-width apart, knees slightly bent, back straight, arms hanging relaxed at the sides.

2) Turn your palms up with the fingers of the hands point towards each other.

3) Inhale, allowing your belly to expand and your arms to move apart at about waist height. Bring your attention to your elbows as you do so, so that they lead the movement of your arms. Observe the movement of both hands with your peripheral vision.

6) Bring your arms to the starting position and repeat from 2).

5) Exhale and bring your arms towards each other, maintaining the feeling of extending outwards.

4) Hold your breath briefly as your palms rotate towards the floor. Extend your mind along the line of your arms and beyond, keeping your shoulder joints open but relaxed.

Preparatory exercise

Breathing exercise #2

In this breathing exercise, you focus on your elbows leading the up and down movement of your arms, and initiate these movements with a slight raising and lowering of your centre.

1) Stand with the feet about shoulder-width apart, knees slightly bent, back straight, arms hanging relaxed at the sides.

2) Inhale, straighten your legs and after a tiny delay raise your arms as if your elbows were being drawn upwards. Your hands and shoulders should be relaxed.

3) Lift your arms to about shoulder height.

6) Return to the starting position, completely relax your arms and repeat several times.

5) Bend your knees, breath out and after a tiny delay lower your arms to waist height.

4) Keeping your wrists at the same height drop your elbows and raise your fingers so that your palms are facing forward.

Preparatory exercise

Breathing exercise #3
In this breathing exercise you open your shoulder joints and perform a quick inhalation and long, slow exhalation.

1) Stand with the feet about shoulder-width apart, knees slightly bent, back straight, arms hanging relaxed at the sides.

2) Cross your hands at the wrists and start straighten your legs just before you begin a quick inhalation and raise your arms.

3) On completion of your full inhalation your arms are extended above your head. Pause your breath briefly.

4) Bend your knees, breath out and move your arms apart over your head.

6) Return to the starting position and repeat several times.

5) Slowly lower your arms. Keep the shoulder joints open and expand your arms outwards observing their movement with your peripheral vision.

Junbi taiso

Junbi Taiso is the term often used for preparatory warming-up exercises. Here we describe some typical stretching exercises.

Arm swinging

1) With your legs apart, knees slightly bent, keep your hips facing forward throughout the exercise. Your back should be straight and your arms relaxed. Using the rotation of your hips, swing your fully relaxed arms to one side…

2) …and then to the other side. Repeat several times.

Preparatory exercise

Side stretch

1) With your legs apart, knees slightly bent, keep your hips facing forward throughout the exercise. Your back should be straight and your arms relaxed.

2) With your legs apart, reach up with your right arm, opening the shoulder joint, as you inhale. Exhale and stretch to the left side with your weight on your right leg and your hips facing forward.

3) Inhale and reach up with your left arm. Exhale and stretch to the other side, with your weight on your right left leg and again with your hips facing forward.

Back bend

1) With your legs apart, knees slightly bent, keep your hips facing forward throughout the exercise. Your back should be straight and your arms relaxed.

2) Exhaling, bend forward from the waist keeping your legs straight. Touch the floor between your feet.

3) Straighten up as you inhale and…

4) …exhale as you arch your back and look behind you. Again, keep your legs straight. And then relax back into the starting position before doing it all over again…

38

Back rotation

1) With your legs wide apart, exhale and bend forward from the waist. Touch the mat with the tips of your fingers

2) Inhale and swing your arms to the left.

3) Still inhaling bend backwards.

4) Exhale and bend to the side.

5) Still exhaling, touch the mat with the tips of your fingers.

Leg stretch 1

1) Adopting a wide posture, turn to the right and bend your front knee. Keep your left leg straight and keep the whole sole of your left foot in contact with the floor. Breathe out as you stretch.

2) Repeat on the other side.

Leg stretch 2

1) Adopting a wide posture, turn to the left and bend your right knee. Keep your left leg straight, toes of the left foot raised and keep the whole sole of your right foot in contact with the floor. Breathe out as you stretch.

2) Repeat on the other side.

Hip Stretch

With your feet flat on the mat bend your knees and squat down to your full extent. Keep your back as vertical as possible and use your elbows to maintain your shins as vertical as possible.

Wrist exercises

These exercises help to strengthen your wrists and make them flexible in preparation for *tekubi waza* (hand/wrist techniques).

Nikyo #1

1) With your hands at about chest height have your palms facing down.

2) Place your right hand over your left and grasp it firmly.

3) Close your armpits so that your elbows move together stretching your left wrist.

Nikyo #2

1) Stretch your arms in front of you with the back of your left hand facing the palm of your right hand.

2) Grasp your left hand with your right hand.

3) Keeping your left elbow as low as possible, draw the little finger of your left hand close to your nose.

Sankyo

1) Stretch your arms in front of you and turn your right hand so that the palm is facing forward.

2) Grasp your right hand with your left hand. Use your left hand to twist your right hand so that the little finger moves towards your right armpit.

Kotegaeshi

1) Take hold of the underside of your left hand with your right hand and bend your left wrist. The thumb of your right hand will be at the base of the little finger of your left hand and the little finger of your right hand will be at the base of the thumb of your left hand.

2) Lower your hands to about waist height twisting your left wrist away from you.

Atemi

In *Aikido atemi* is practised for a number of reasons. Firstly, in order to learn how to defend ourselves from such attacks, our *Aikido* partners need to be able to deliver them effectively. Secondly, *atemi* can be used to distract an opponent to provide an opening for an *Aikido* technique. Thirdly, in *atemi* practice we learn basic body movements that we use in the execution of *Aikido* techniques. Fourthly, when practised with a partner, *atemi* practise gives us an awareness of correct distance between *uke* and *tori*. Finally, although ideally in *Aikido* our intention is not to seriously injure our attackers, under certain circumstances that could be life threatening, such as being attacked with a knife, powerful *atemi* may need to be used to disable the attacker.

The exercises shown in this section can be practised solo or with a partner as illustrated.

Shomen uchi

This is a vertical strike to the top of the opponent's head.

1) Start with your right leg forward. Raise your right hand so that your wrist is just above the top of your head.

2) Move forward to within striking distance as you swing your arm in an outward arc. The edge of your right hand swings towards the top of *uke's* head with the aim of cutting through to about waist height.

Yokomen uchi

This is a strike to the side of the opponent's head.

1) Start with your left leg forward. Raise your right hand so that the valley between your thumb and index finger touch the centre of your forehead at about the hair line. Move your elbow to the side to open the shoulder joint.

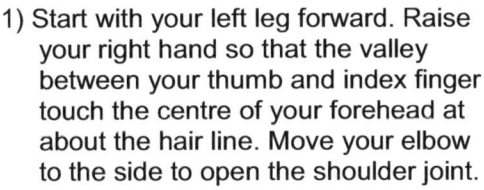

2) Step diagonally forward on your right leg and swing your arm in an arc as your left leg moves behind your right leg. The edge of your right hand swings across your upper body to the side of *uke's* head.

Chudan tsuki

This is a straight punch. The strike described here is to the mid-section but the same general action can be directed towards the head (*jodan tsuki*) or to below the waist (*gedan tsuki*)

1) Start with your left leg forward and your right fist at the side of your waist.

2) Without changing the positions of your arms step forward on your right leg but maintain the majority of your body weight on your left leg.

3) Transfer your weight forward and as your right knee bends strike horizontally with your right fist and withdraw your left hand to your waist ready to repeat on the other side.

Jodan tsuki

This is a straight punch. The strike described here is to the head but the same general action can be directed towards the mid-section (*chudan tsuki*) or to below the waist (*gedan tsuki*).

1) Start with your left leg forward and your right fist at the side of your waist.

2) Without changing the positions of your arms step forward on your right leg but maintain the majority of your body weight on your left leg.

3) Transfer your weight forward and as your right knee bends strike towards *uke's* head with your right fist and withdraw your left hand to your waist ready to repeat on the other side.

Tori fune and Furitama

Tori fune, sometimes called the 'rowing exercise' requires you to coordinate your breathing with the transference of your body weight forwards and backwards, and with the extension and retraction of your arms. This is an ideal way to practice 'body first, then arms'.

Traditionally *tori fune* is followed by a shaking exercise called *furitama*. The hands are clasped together firmly and are alternately extended downwards and then relaxed. The movement is performed vigorously to make the whole body shake. Your awareness is moved to your *hara*.

Tori fune

1) Start with your left leg forward, bent at the knee, your right leg straight and your arms extended at about waist height. Inhale.

2) Without changing the positions of your arms transfer your weight to your rear leg…

3) …just before you exhale and withdraw your hands to the sides of your waist.

4) Inhale. Move your weight forward to your left leg…

5) …just before you exhale and thrust your arms forward. Ensure both feet remain flat on the floor.

Furitama

Clasp your hands together firmly and bend your knees slightly. Have your eyes closed and your back straight. Extend your arms towards the floor, straightening your elbows. Keep your shoulders relaxed. Imagine that your hands are wet and you are flicking water downwards. Then relax your arms and lift your arms up slightly before repeating vigorously.

Shikko

Shikko, or knee walking, is a practice that is very typically included in *Aikido* training sessions. It develops an acute awareness of centre and the ability to move from the hips quickly and efficiently.

Suwari waza no Shikko

1) Start by sitting on your heels with your toes tucked under. Lift your right knee and move your right leg forward. Follow the movement of your right foot with your left foot so that your feet stay close together.

2) Drop your right knee to the floor and bring your left knee forward.

3) Drop your left knee to the floor and bring your right knee forward.

Ukemi

Half of *Aikido* practice requires taking *ukemi*, that is breakfalls. You need to be confident that you won't be injured when your partner performs a technique with you, so it is important to practice *ukemi* regularly until you can roll confidently and without discomfort. The two major forms of *ukemi* are *mae ukemi* (forward roll) and *ushiro ukemi* (backward roll).

Mae ukemi

1) Start close to the mat with your right knee down and your left knee up. Place your right palm on the mat.

2) Straighten your left right so that you begin to topple forward. Extend you left arm towards the gap between your right arm and your right leg.

3) Exhale and push yourself forward turning slightly to your right so that the outside surface of your left arm and the back of your left shoulder make light contact with the mat.

4) Roll over with the toes of your right foot tucked under so that you can stand up easily.

After becoming confident rolling from the kneeling position, repeat the same sequence but starting from standing:

Preparatory exercise

Ushiro ukemi

1) Start close to the mat with your right knee down and your left knee up.

2) Sit back slightly to the right just behind your right foot.

3) Exhale and push yourself backwards rolling over your left shoulder.

4) Use your hands to push yourself up.

5) Move your right leg forward and stand up.

Part 3: Tai sabaki

Tai sabaki, or body movements, form the foundation of *Aikido* techniques. They allow you to move to the right place at the right time to assume strategically strong positions relative to your attacker. They are combined in various ways during the execution of techniques and thus are major building blocks upon which *Aikido* practice is based.

Aikido classes almost invariably include solo or paired exercises to rehearse and refine the basic *tai sabaki* and it is generally accepted that they are essential to *Aikido* training. All of the *tai sabaki* described in this part of the book are important components of the techniques described in Part 4, so practising them until they are 'in your body' is central to mastering *Aikido*.

Kaiten: change direction 180°

Starting in *hidari-hanmi* (left posture) you pivot on the balls of both feet so that you turn clockwise 180° into *migi-hanmi* (right posture) facing the opposite direction. This movement is often combined with other basic *tai sabaki* forms in the execution of such techniques as *ikkyo (ura)*, *irimi-nage* and *shiho-nage*.

1) Start in *hidari-hanmi*

2) Turn 180° clockwise into *migi-hanmi*

Irimi-ashi: step forward

This is an entering movement in which you step forward on the rear foot and then turn the body through a small angle to move off the direct line of attack.

1) Start in *hidari-hanmi*.

2) *Irimi*. Step forward on your rear foot by pushing off from your front leg.

3) *Han-tenkan*. Turn your hips about 30° and adjust your rear leg position.

Yoko-ashi: step to the side

This is a simple step to the side retaining the same posture. The step can be to the left or to the right depending on the circumstances.

1) Start in *hidari-hanmi*.

2) Move to the side leading with the left leg.

Okuri-ashi: step forward, front leg leading

(also referred to as **Tsuki-ashi**)

Move forward on your front foot, widening the posture and adjust the posture width to normal by following with the rear foot. Moving backwards, the rear leg begins the movement. A variation involves beginning the movement by moving the rear leg towards the front leg followed by the front leg stepping forward. Again, the whole body moves forward.

1) Start in *hidari-hanmi*.

2) Move your front foot forward, followed by the rear foot, so that you end in the same posture as before.

Tenkan: full turn

In this important movement you turn 180° (*kaiten*) and then step back (*ushiro-ashi*). This movement is a major component of many *Aikido* techniques.

1) Start in *migi-hanmi*.

2) Turn the hips 180° turning on the balls of the feet (*kaiten*). The right arm swings forward in a vertical arc.

3) Step back keeping on your left leg most of your weight on the front leg which is bent at the knee.

Paired exercise

Tai sabaki

Han-tenkan: half/small turn

This is a partial rotation about the front foot, that is less than a full turn.

1) Start in hidari-hanmi.

2) Turn the hips about 90°, turning on the balls of the feet. Most of your weight is on the front leg which is bent at the knee.

Sokumen: step to the side and turn

Step to the side and turn approximately 90°. This movement, and its variations, are used in the execution of a range of techniques.

1) Start in *hidari-hanmi*.

2) Move the left leg to the left and the right foot to the position the left foot formerly occupied, changing direction by 90°.

Paired exercise

Ushiro-sokumen: step back and turn

Step diagonally back and adjust posture. This movement is used when there is a lot of forward energy in the attack, as with *chudan-tsuki*. It takes you off the line of attack and makes distance between you and your attacker.

1) Start in *hidari-hanmi*.

2) Move your left foot diagonally back to the left and retract your right foot to establish *migi-hanmi*.

Paired exercise

Irimi-sokumen: DIAGONAL STEP FORWARD, SIDE TURN

Step diagonally forward and turn.

1) Start in *migi-hanmi*.

2) Step forward and to the left on the left foot.

3) Adjust the right leg for *migi-hanmi*.

Paired exercise

Irimi-tenkan: step forward, full turn

Step forward (*irimi*), turn about 180° and step back (*tenkan*). This movement, one of the most important forms of Aikido *tai-sabaki*, enables you to combine a large forward movement with a powerful hip rotation. The *tenkan* component of the movement can be a full 180° turn or any smaller angle (*han-tenkan*) depending on the technique being performed.

1) Start in migi-hanmi.

2) Step forward on rear (left) foot and turn 180°.

3) Step back into *hidari-hanmi*.

Paired exercise

Irimi hantenkan: step diagonally forward, small turn

Step diagonally forward (*irimi*), and adjust the rear foot position (*han-tenkan*). This movement is used in techniques such as *yokomen uchi shiho nage*.

1) Start in *hidari-hanmi*.

2) *Irimi*. Step diagonally forward on your rear foot by pushing off from your front leg.

3) *Han-tenkan*. Adjust your rear leg position.

Paired exercise

Uke attacks with *yokomen uchi* and you intercept the attack while moving in front of her with *irimi hantenkan*. *Uke* then immediately attacks with the other arm, and so on.

Tai sabaki

Three attacks exercise

In this exercise *uke* attacks *tori* with *shomen uchi*, followed by *yokomen uchi*, followed by *chudan tsuki*. *Tori* performs various *tai sabaki* to avoid the attacks and to move to a safe position.

1) *Uke* attacks *shomen uchi* with her left arm.

2) You intercept the attack with *irimi-tenkan*...

3) ... and step back. *Uke* steps forward and turns, preparing to attack *yokomen uchi* with her right arm.

4) *Uke* attacks *yokomen uchi* and you intercept stepping diagonally forward with *irimi hantenkan* (halfturn).

5) *Uke* attacks *chudan tsuki* with her left arm.

6) You intercept the attack and pivot on your leading foot, turning 180° (*tenkan*). You then step back.

7) *Tori* steps back again as *uke* steps forward and turns, preparing to attack *shomen uchi* with her right arm. The sequence repeats but with *uke* attacking alternately right and left *shomen uchi*, *yokomen uchi* and *chudan tsuki*.

Part 4: Kihon Waza

In this part of the book we describe seven commonly practised techniques and relate each of them to a number of the *tai-sabaki* forms described in Part 3. For each technique, we describe variations for two classes of attacks:

Katate dori

- *gyaku hanmi katate dori*
- *ai hanmi katate dori (kosa dori)*

Uchi

- *shomen-uchi*
- *yokomen-uchi*
- *chudan-tsuki*
- *jodan-tsuki*

The two *katate-dori* forms can be practised as preparatory exercises for the *uchi* attacks listed above or as independent techniques.

Practice recommendations

We recommend that you follow the guidelines below in order to obtain the maximum benefit from your training. This is particularly important if you have not been practising *Aikido* for very long.

1. Practice the preparatory (that is the *katate-dori*) forms slowly and carefully, paying particular attention to *tai-sabaki*, until the shape of the technique is in your body and you can perform each part of it accurately.
2. After you are comfortable with the preparatory form, continue to practice it slowly but make it smooth and continuous with no stops and starts.
3. The next stage is to get the technique up to practical speed, but without losing any of the detail.
4. Introduce *leading* once the technique has been thoroughly practised as suggested above. In this stage you don't allow your partner to establish a strong grip, or you avoid his contact altogether. Your wrist becomes bait that will lead your partner to a position that gives you a strategic advantage.
5. Progress to the strike attack, again starting slowly and carefully and ensuring that correct *tai-sabaki* is observed. The *tai-sabaki* throughout the execution of the technique should be almost identical to that of the preparatory form.
6. Finally bring the technique up to practical speed, with your partner attacking you with full commitment.

Ikkyo

Ikkyo is an arm control technique and forms the basis of several other important techniques such as *Nikyo* and *Sankyo*. Appearing simply a matter of grabbing *uke's* arm at the wrist and elbow, it is in fact technically quite difficult to execute effectively. However, it is worth your perseverance since it can be used to deal with any form of attack, and the principles it employs are appropriate to a wide range of other *Aikido* techniques.

The table below shows the *Ikkyo* variations described in this section of the book. The *kosa dori* and *katate dori* forms are techniques in themselves but they also serve as preparation for more difficult attacks such as *shomen uchi, yokomen uchi* and *tsuki*.

Attack	*Form*
Kosa dori	Yoko ashi omote
Kosa dori	Yoko ashi ura
Shomen uchi	Yoko ashi omote
Shomen uchi	Yoko ashi ura
Jodan tsuki	Yoko ashi omote
Jodan tsuki	Yoko ashi ura
Katate dori	Ushiro sokumen omote
Katate dori	Ushiro sokumen ura
Chudan tsuki	Ushiro sokumen omote
Chudan tsuki	Ushiro sokumen ura
Kosa dori	Irimi sokumen ura
Chudan tsuki	Irimi sokumen ura

Kosa dori Ikkyo omote #1

In this *Ikkyo uke* attacks with *kosa dori (ai-hanmi katate dori)*. You step to the side (*yoko ashi*) in front of *uke* as you execute the technique. This form of *Ikkyo* is also a preparation for *shomen uchi* and *jodan tsuki* attacks.

1) *Uke* attacks with *kosa dori*.

2) You step to the side (*yoko ashi*) as you swing your right hand up drawing *uke* off-balance.

3) Leading with the elbow, your right forearm aligns with his arm as you turn to the right and your left hand takes hold just above the elbow.

6) Kneel down, sitting on your heels, feet together and pin *uke's* arm. Your right hand controls his wrist and your left hand presses his elbow and shoulder to the mat.

5) Lead *uke* down to the mat keeping his arm straight.

4) Drop both of your hands down to waist height.

Ikkyo

Kosa dori Ikkyo ura #1

In this *Ikkyo uke* attacks with *kosa dori (ai-hanmi katate dori)*. You step to the side (*yoko ashi*) and behind *uke* as you execute the technique. This form of *Ikkyo* is also a preparation for *shomen uchi* and *jodan tsuki* attacks.

1) *Uke* attacks with *kosa dori*.

2) You swing your arm up, reach for his elbow, step to the side and turn your hips so that you are facing in the same direction as *uke*.

5) Kneel down, sitting on your heels, feet together, and pin *uke's* arm. Your right hand controls his wrist and your left hand presses his elbow and shoulder to the mat.

4) Turn 180° and drop your hands to waist height. Lead *uke* down to the mat keeping his arm straight.

3) Step back keeping your arms at about shoulder height, drawing *uke* off-balance.

Shomen uchi Ikkyo omote #1

In this *Ikkyo uke* attacks with *shomen uchi*. You step to the side (*yoko ashi*) in front of *uke* as you execute the technique.

1) *Uke* attacks with *shomen uchi*.

2) You step to the right (*yoko ashi*) as you swing your right hand up to intercept the striking arm.

3) You turn to the right and your left hand takes hold just above the elbow.

6) Kneel down, sitting on your heels, feet together, and pin *uke's* arm. Your right hand controls his wrist and your left hand presses his elbow and shoulder to the mat.

5) Lead *uke* down to the mat keeping his arm straight.

4) Drop both of your hands down to waist height.

Shomen uchi Ikkyo ura #1

In this *Ikkyo uke* attacks with *shomen uchi*. You step to the side (*yoko ashi*) and behind *uke* as you execute the technique.

1) *Uke* attacks with *shomen uchi*.

2) You swing your arm up to intercept his attack, reach for his elbow, step to the side and turn your hips so that you are facing in the same direction as *uke*.

4) Kneel down, sitting on your heels, feet together and pin *uke's* arm. Your right hand controls his wrist and your left hand presses his elbow and shoulder to the mat.

3) Step back and turn 180° keeping your arms at about shoulder height, drawing *uke* off-balance. Drop your hands to waist height. Lead *uke* down to the mat.

Jodan tsuki Ikkyo omote

In this *Ikkyo uke* attacks with *jodan tsuki*. You step to the side (*yoko ashi*) in front of *uke* as you execute the technique.

1) *Uke* attacks with *jodan tsuki*.

2) You step to the side (*yoko ashi*) as you swing your right hand up to intercept and deflect the striking arm. You take hold of his wrist as you turn to the right and your left hand takes hold just above the elbow.

6) Kneel down, sitting on your heels, feet together, and pin *uke's* arm. Your right hand controls his wrist and your left hand presses his elbow and shoulder to the mat.

5) Lead *uke* down to the mat keeping his arm straight.

4) Drop both of your hands down to waist height.

Jodan tsuki Ikkyo ura

In this *Ikkyo uke* attacks with *jodan tsuki*. You step to the side and behind *uke* as you execute the technique.

1) *Uke* attacks with *jodan tsuki*.

2) You swing your arm up to intercept his attack, reach for his elbow, step to the side and turn your hips so that you are facing in the same direction as *uke*. Your right hand takes hold of his wrist.

5) Kneel down, sitting on your heels, feet together and pin *uke's* arm. Your right hand controls his wrist and your left hand presses his elbow and shoulder to the mat.

4) Turn 180° and drop your hands to waist height. Lead *uke* down to the mat keeping his arm straight.

3) Pivot on your left (rear) foot keeping your arms at about shoulder height and drawing *uke* off-balance.

Katate dori Ikkyo omote #1

In this *Ikkyo uke* attacks with *katate dori*. You step back diagonally to the side (*ushiro sokumen*) as you execute the technique. This form of *Ikkyo* is also a good preparation for *chudan tsuki* attacks.

1) *Uke* attacks with *katate dori*.

2) You step back diagonally to the side (*ushiro sokumen*) drawing *uke's* weight to his front leg. Your right hand moves across to take hold of the back of his right hand.

3) You disengage your held (left) hand, turn your hips to the right and take hold just above the elbow with your left hand.

6) Kneel down, sitting on your heels, feet together, and pin *uke's* arm. Your right hand controls his wrist and your left hand presses his elbow and shoulder to the mat.

5) Lead *uke* down to the mat keeping his arm straight.

4) Drop both of your hands down to waist height and step forward on your left leg.

Katate dori Ikkyo ura #1

In this *Ikkyo uke* attacks with *katate dori*. You step back diagonally to the side (*ushiro sokumen*) and then move behind *uke*. This form of *Ikkyo* is also a good preparation for *chudan tsuki* attacks.

1) *Uke* attacks with *katate dori*.

2) You step back diagonally to the side (*ushiro sokumen*) drawing *uke's* weight to his front leg. Your right hand moves across to take hold of the back of his right hand.

3) You disengage your held (left) hand and take hold just above the elbow with your left hand.

6) Kneel down, sitting on your heels, feet together, and pin *uke's* arm. Your right hand controls his wrist and your left hand presses his elbow and shoulder to the mat.

5) Step back on your right leg and turn your hips 180° to the right leading *uke* down to the mat.

4) Step deeply to *uke's* rear on your left leg and begin to turn to your right, extending him off-balance.

Chudan tsuki Ikkyo omote

In this *Ikkyo uke* attacks with *chudan tsuki*. You step back diagonally to the side (*ushiro sokumen*) as you intercept the attack and execute the technique.

1) Uke attacks with chudan tsuki.

2) You step back diagonally to the side (*ushiro sokumen*) intercepting *uke's* punch and drawing his weight to his front leg. Your right hand moves across to take hold of the back of his right hand.

5) Kneel down, sitting on your heels, feet together, and pin *uke's* arm. Your right hand controls his wrist and your left hand presses his elbow and shoulder to the mat.

4) Lead *uke* down to the mat keeping his arm straight.

3) You turn your hips to the right and take hold just above the elbow with your left hand.

Ikkyo

Chudan tsuki Ikkyo ura

In this *Ikkyo uke* attacks with *chudan tsuki*. You step back diagonally to the side (*ushiro sokumen*) as you intercept the attack and execute the technique.

1) Uke attacks with chudan tsuki.

2) You step back diagonally to the side (*ushiro sokumen*) intercepting *uke's* punch and drawing his weight to his front leg. Your right hand moves across to take hold of the back of his right hand.

4) Kneel down, sitting on your heels, feet together, and pin *uke's* arm. Your right hand controls his wrist and your left hand presses his elbow and shoulder to the mat.

3) Step deeply to *uke's* rear on your left leg and continue to turn to your right, extending him off-balance. Lead *uke* down to the mat keeping his arm straight. You turn your hips to the right and take hold just above the elbow with your left hand.

Ikkyo

Kosa dori Ikkyo ura #2

In this *Ikkyo uke* attacks with *kosa dori (ai-hanmi katate dori)*. You step forward and to the side behind *uke* (*irimi sokumen*) as you execute the technique. This form of *Ikkyo* is also a preparation for *chudan tsuki* attacks.

1) *Uke* attacks with *kosa dori*.

2) You step diagonally forward on your left leg to the side and rear of *uke*, at the same time leading him forward onto his front leg.

3) You swing your arm up as you take a small step forward on your right leg.

6) Kneel down, sitting on your heels, feet together and pin *uke's* arm. Your right hand controls his wrist and your left hand presses his elbow and shoulder to the mat.

5) As *uke* begins to fall in front of you, step back on your left leg, turn your hips and lead him down to the mat keeping his arm straight.

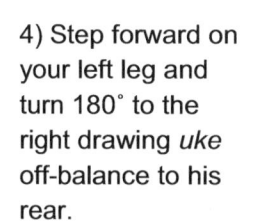

4) Step forward on your left leg and turn 180° to the right drawing *uke* off-balance to his rear.

Chudan tsuki Ikkyo ura #2

In this *Ikkyo uke* attacks with *chudan tsuki*. You step forward and to the side behind *uke* (*irimi sokumen*) as you execute the technique.

1) *Uke* attacks with *chudan tsuki*.

2) You step diagonally forward on your left leg to the side and rear of *uke*, at the same time leading him forward onto his front leg with your right hand making contact with his attacking (right) arm. You swing your right arm up as you take a small step forward on your right leg. Your left hand begins to move towards his elbow.

5) Kneel down, sitting on your heels, feet together and pin *uke's* arm. Your right hand controls his wrist and your left hand presses his elbow and shoulder to the mat.

4) As *uke* begins to fall in front of you, step back on your left leg, turn your hips and lead him down to the mat keeping his arm straight.

3) Grasp *uke's* elbow with your left hand, step forward on your left leg and turn 180° to the right drawing *uke* off-balance to his rear.

Ikkyo

Nikyo

Nikyo is classed as *tekubi waza*, a hand control technique. It is a very powerful wrist lock that can be applied as a technique in its own right or as a response to *uke* resisting another technique such as *Ikkyo*.

The table below shows the *Nikyo* variations described in this section of the book. The *kosa dori* and *katate dori* forms are techniques in themselves but they also serve as preparation for more difficult attacks such as *shomen uchi, yokomen uchi* and *tsuki*.

Attack	*Form*
Kosa dori	Yoko ashi omote
Kosa dori	Yoko ashi ura
Shomen uchi	Yoko ashi omote
Shomen uchi	Yoko ashi ura
Katate dori	Ushiro sokumen omote
Katate dori	Ushiro sokumen ura
Yokomen uchi	Sokumen omote
Yokomen uchi	Sokumen ura

Nikyo

Kosa dori Nikyo omote

In this *Nikyo uke* attacks with *kosa dori (ai-hanmi katate dori)*. You step to the side in front of *uke* as you execute the technique. This form of *Nikyo* is also a preparation for *shomen uchi* and *jodan tsuki* attacks.

1) *Uke* attacks with *kosa dori*.

2) You swing your arm up and step to the side (*yoko ashi*).

3) Turning your hips to the right you grasp *uke's* arm at wrist and elbow and draw him off-balance.

4) Drop your hands to waist height as *uke* falls forward.

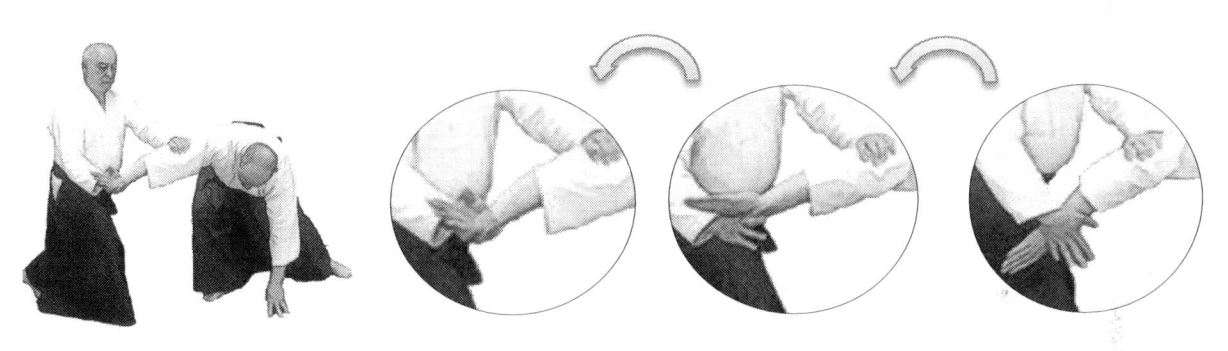

5) Rotate your hand around *uke's* wrist to establish the *Nikyo* control.

6) Control *uke's* shoulder as you prepare to immobilise him. Align his arm with yours and trap his wrist in your elbow crease, the edge of your other hand drawing his elbow to your waist.

7) Place the back of *uke's* hand on the base of his spine and your other hand on the side of his face before you stand up.

Kosa dori Nikyo ura

In this *Nikyo uke* attacks with *kosa dori (ai-hanmi katate dori)*. You step to the side and behind *uke* as you execute the technique. This form of *Nikyo* is also a preparation for *shomen uchi* and *jodan tsuki* attacks.

1) *Uke* attacks with *kosa dori*.

2) You swing your arm up, step to *uke's* side and grasp his elbow with your free hand.

3) Swinging both arms down you pivot on your right foot (*tenkan*).

4) As *uke* attempts to regain his balance you slide your right hand to his wrist, release your left hand from his grip and take hold of his hand…

7) Control *uke's* shoulder as you prepare to immobilise him.

6) You then take hold of *uke's* elbow with you right hand and take him down to the mat.

5) … and apply the wrist control to cause *uke* to drop down to his knees.

8) Align his arm with yours and trap his wrist in your elbow crease, the edge of your other hand drawing is elbow to your waist. Lift up and turn to complete the control.

9) Place the back of *uke's* hand on the base of his spine and your other hand on the side of his face before you stand up.

Shomen uchi Nikyo omote

In this *Nikyo uke* attacks with *shomen uchi*. You step to the side in front of *uke* as you execute the technique.

1) *Uke* attacks with *shomen uchi*.

2) You swing your arms up and step to the side (*yoko ashi*) intercepting the attack.

3) Turning your hips to the left you grasp *uke's* arm at wrist and elbow and draw him off-balance by dropping your hands to waist height.

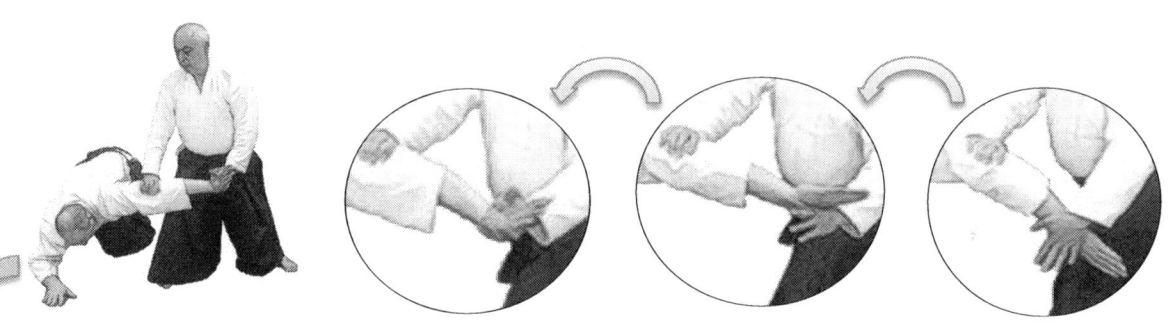

4) Rotate your hand around *uke's* wrist to establish the *Nikyo* control.

5) Control *uke's* shoulder as you prepare to immobilise him. Align his arm with yours and trap his wrist in your elbow crease, the edge of your other hand drawing his elbow to your waist.

6) Place the back of *uke's* hand on the base of his spine and your other hand on the side of his face before you stand up.

Shomen uchi Nikyo ura

In this *Nikyo uke* attacks with *shomen uchi*. You step to the side of *uke* as you execute the technique.

1) *Uke* attacks with *shomen uchi*.

2) You swing your arms up, intercepting *uke's* attack, and step to the side (*yoko ashi*).

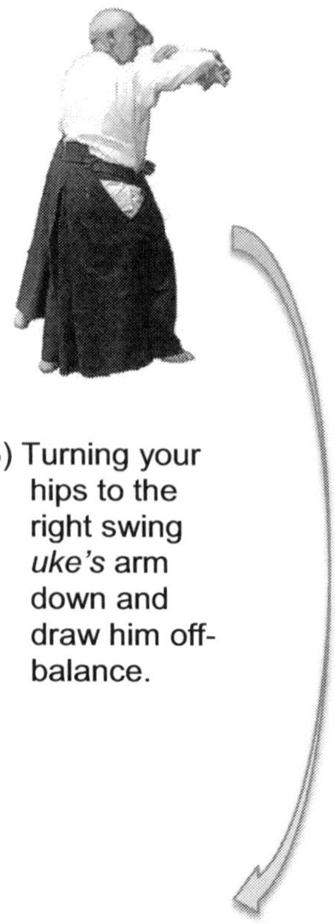

3) Turning your hips to the right swing *uke's* arm down and draw him off-balance.

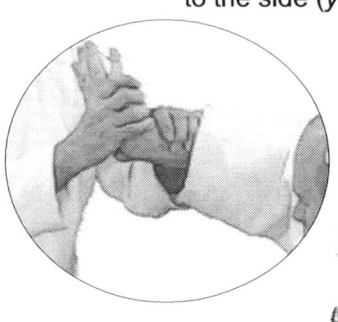

5) Release your left hand grip and take *uke* face down to the mat.

4) As *uke* attempts to regain his balance establish the *Nikyo* control.

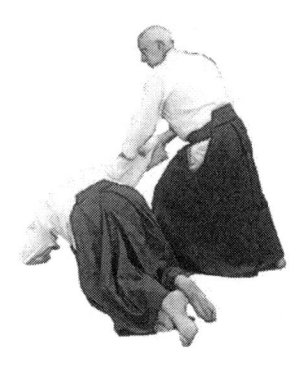

6) Control *uke's* shoulder as you prepare to immobilise him. Align his arm with yours and trap his wrist in your elbow crease.

7) The edge of your other hand draws his elbow to your waist.

Katate dori Nikyo omote

In this *Nikyo uke* attacks with *katate dori (gyaku-hanmi)*. You step to the side and back (*ushiro sokumen*) as you execute the technique. This form of *Nikyo* is also a preparation for *chudan tsuki* attacks.

1) *Uke* attacks with *katate dori*.

2) Step to the side and slightly back to draw *uke's* weight onto his leading leg. Take hold of the back of his hand with your free hand.

3) Swing his arm up as you release your grasped hand to take hold of his elbow.

4) Swing both hand down in front of you to break *uke's* balance.

5) Take him down to the mat.

6) Control *uke's* shoulder as you prepare to immobilise him.

7) Align his arm with yours and trap his wrist in your elbow crease, the edge of your other hand drawing is elbow to your waist. Lift up and turn to complete the control.

8) Place the back of *uke's* hand on the base of his spine and your other hand on the side of his face before you stand up.

Katate dori Nikyo ura

In this *Nikyo uke* attacks with *katate dori (gyaku-hanmi*. You step to the side and back (*sokumen*) as you execute the technique. This form of *Nikyo* is also a preparation for *chudan tsuki* attacks.

1) *Uke* attacks with *katate dori*.

2) Step to the side and slightly back to draw *uke's* weight onto his leading leg. Take hold of the back of his hand with your free hand.

3) Swing his arm up as you release your grasped hand to take hold of his elbow and step to his side.

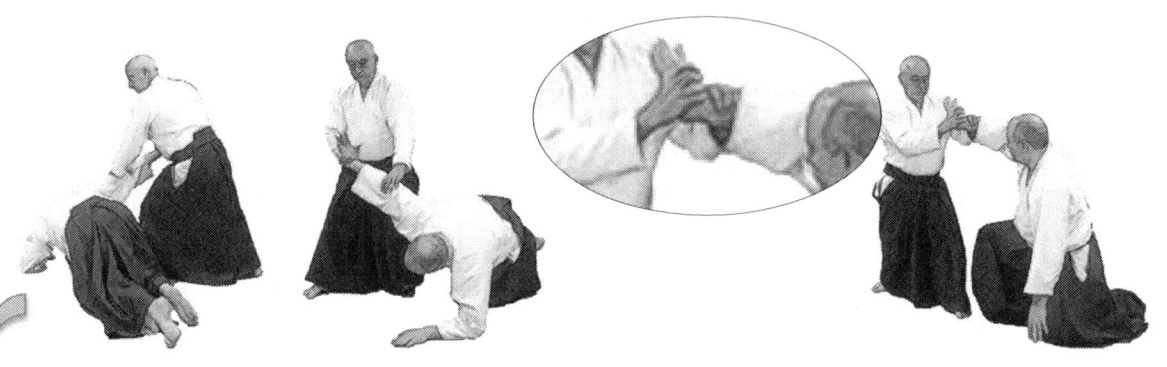

5) Pivoting on your left foot take hold of his elbow and lead him down to the mat.

4) Swing both hand down in front of and step back. *Uke* will turn and fall to his knees in front of you. The hand at *uke's* elbow slides down to his wrist and you apply the *Nikyo* control.

6) *Align his arm with yours and trap his wrist in your elbow crease, the edge of your other hand drawing is elbow to your waist. Your knees sandwich his shoulder. Lift up and turn to complete the control.*

Yokomen uchi Nikyo omote

In this *Nikyo uke* attacks with *katate dori (gyaku-hanmi*. You step to the side of *uke* (*sokumen*) as you execute the technique.

1) *Uke* attacks with *katate dori*.

2) Step to the side and slightly back to draw *uke's* weight onto his leading leg. Take hold of the back of his hand with your free hand.

3) Swing his arm up as you release your grasped hand to take hold of his elbow.

5) Take him down to the mat.

4) Swing both hand down in front of you to break *uke's* balance.

6) Control *uke's* shoulder as you prepare to immobilise him. Align his arm with yours and trap his wrist in your elbow crease, the edge of your other hand drawing is elbow to your waist. Lift up and turn to complete the control.

7) Place the back of uke's hand on the base of his spine and your other hand on the side of his face before you stand up.

Yokomen uchi Nikyo ura

In this *Nikyo uke* attacks with *yokomen uchi*. You step to the side of *uke* (*sokumen*) and then behind as you execute the technique.

1) *Uke* attacks with *yokomen uchi*.

2) Step to the side, intercepting his attack with your extended arm, palm up.

3) Your right hand makes contact with the underside of *uke's* wrist.

5) Pivoting on your left foot take hold of his elbow and lead him down to the mat.

4) Step forward and turn, taking hold of *uke's* wrist. *Uke* will turn to face you. Take hold of the back of his hand with your other hand and apply the *Nikyo* control.

6) Align his arm with yours and trap his wrist in your elbow crease, the edge of your other hand drawing is elbow to your waist. Your knees sandwich his shoulder. Lift up and turn to complete the control.

Sankyo

Sankyo

Sankyo is classed as *tekubi waza*, a hand control technique. It is a very powerful wrist lock that can be applied as a technique in its own right or as a response to *uke* resisting another technique such as *Ikkyo*.

The table below shows the *Sankyo* variations described in this section of the book. The *kosa dori* and *katate dori* forms are techniques in themselves but they also serve as preparation for more difficult attacks such as *shomen uchi, yokomen uchi* and *tsuki*.

Attack	*Form*
Kosa dori	*Yoko ashi omote*
Kosa dori	*Yoko ashi ura*
Shomen uchi	*Yoko ashi omote*
Shomen uchi	*Yoko ashi ura*
Jodan tsuki	*Yoko ashi omote*
Jodan tsuki	*Yoko ashi ura*
Katate dori	*Sokumen omote*
Katate dori	*Sokumen ura*
Yokomen uchi	*Sokumen omote*
Yokomen uchi	*Sokumen ura*
Katate dori	*Ushiro sokumen omote*
Katate dori	*Ushiro sokumen ura*
Chudan tsuki	*Ushiro sokumen omote*
Chudan tsuki	*Ushiro sokumen ura*

Kosa dori Sankyo omote

In this *Sankyo uke* attacks with *kosa dori (ai-hanmi katate dori)*. You step to the side (*yoko ashi*) in front of *uke* to execute the technique. This form of *Sankyo* is also a preparation for *shomen uchi* and *jodan tsuki* attacks.

1) *Uke* attacks with *kosa dori* in *migi hanmi* (right posture).

2) Swing your held arm up as you step to the side (*yoko ashi*) and take hold of her elbow with your free hand.

3) Turn your hips to the right to break *uke*'s balance.

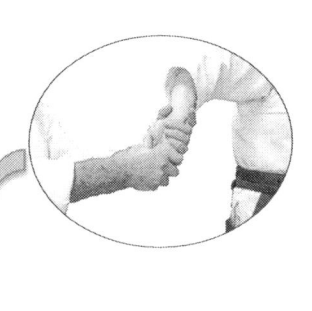

4) Reach under *uke*'s arm and take hold of the side of her hand. Your right hand slides down to capture her fingers and to establish the *Sankyo* control.

5) Direct *uke* to the mat and step forward, taking hold of the inside of her elbow with your right hand.

6) Kneel down and apply the *Sankyo* immobilisation, the knife edge (*tegatana*) of your left hand drawing *uke*'s elbow to your waist.

Kosa dori Sankyo ura

In this *Sankyo uke* attacks with *kosa dori (ai-hanmi katate dori)*. You step to the side and behind *uke* as you execute the technique. This form of *Sankyo* is also a preparation for *shomen uchi* and *jodan tsuki* attacks.

1) *Uke* attacks with *kosa dori* in *hidari hanmi* (left posture)

2) You swing your arm up, take a large step to *uke's* rear, grasp her elbow and turn 180°.

3) Step back on your left leg and reach under her arm with your right hand to establish the *Sankyo* control.

4) Pivoting on your right foot move your left hand to *uke's* elbow and pin her arm to her lower back.

5) Continuing to pivot on your left foot direct *uke* to the mat.

6) Kneel down and control *uke's* arm, your right hand maintaining the *Sankyo* control and your left hand pinning her shoulder to the mat.

7) Move your left hand to *uke's* hand, keeping the *Sankyo* control on, and use the knife edge of your right hand to draw her elbow towards your waist. Lift up slightly and turn your shoulders to the right to complete the pin.

Shomen uchi Sankyo omote

In this *Sankyo uke* attacks with *shomen uchi*. You step to the side (*yoko ashi*) in front of *uke* to execute the technique.

1) *Uke* attacks with *shomen uchi*.

2) Swing your arms up as you step to the side (*yoko ashi*) and intercept her arm with both of yours.

3) Turn your hips to the right and swing your arms down to break *uke's* balance.

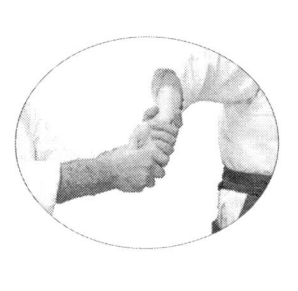

4) Step forward on your left leg and reach under *uke's* arm to take hold of the side of her hand. Your right hand slides down to capture her fingers and establish the *Sankyo* control.

5) Direct *uke* to the mat and step forward, taking hold of the inside of her elbow with your right hand.

6) Kneel down and apply the *Sankyo* immobilisation, the knife edge of your left hand drawing *uke's* elbow to your waist.

Shomen uchi Sankyo ura

In this *Sankyo uke* attacks with *shomen uchi*. You step to the side and behind *uke* as you execute the technique.

1) *Uke* attacks with *shomen uchi*.

2) You swing your arm up to intercept her attack, take a large step to her rear, grasp her elbow and turn 180°.

3) Step back on your left leg and reach under her arm with your right hand to establish the *Sankyo* control.

4) Pivoting on your right foot move your left hand to *uke's* elbow and pin her arm to her lower back.

5) Continuing to pivot on your left foot direct *uke* to the mat.

6) Kneel down and control *uke's* arm, your right hand maintaining the *Sankyo* control and your left hand pinning her shoulder to the mat.

7) Move your left hand to *uke's* hand, keeping the Sankyo control on, and use the knife edge of your right hand to draw her elbow towards your waist. Lift up slightly and turn your shoulders to the right to complete the pin.

Jodan tsuki Sankyo omote

In this *Sankyo uke* attacks with *jodan tsuki*. You step to the side (*yoko ashi*) in front of *uke* to execute the technique.

1) *Uke* attacks with *jodan tsuki*.

2) Swing your arms up as you step to the side (*yoko ashi*) and intercept her arm with both of yours.

3) Turn your hips to the right and swing your arms down to break *uke's* balance.

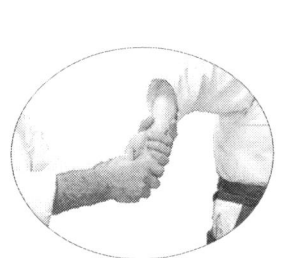

4) Step forward on your left leg and reach under *uke's* arm to take hold of the side of her hand. Your right hand slides down to capture her fingers and establish the *Sankyo* control.

5) Direct *uke* to the mat and step forward, taking hold of the inside of her elbow with your right hand.

6) Kneel down and apply the *Sankyo* immobilisation, the knife edge of your left hand drawing *uke's* elbow to your waist.

Jodan tsuki Sankyo ura

In this *Sankyo uke* attacks with *jodan tsuki*. You step to the side and behind *uke* as you execute the technique.

1) *Uke* attacks with *jodan tsuki*.

2) You swing your arm up to intercept her attack, take a large step to her rear, grasp her elbow and turn 180° swinging her arm down in front of you.

5) Continuing to pivot on your left foot direct *uke* to the mat.

4) Pivoting on your right foot move your left hand to *uke's* elbow and pin her arm to her lower back.

3) Step back on your left leg and reach under her arm with your right hand to establish the *Sankyo* control.

6) Kneel down and control *uke's* arm, your right hand maintaining the *Sankyo* control and your left hand pinning her shoulder to the mat.

7) Move your left hand to *uke's* hand, keeping the Sankyo control on, and use the knife edge of your right hand to draw her elbow towards your waist. Lift up slightly and turn your shoulders to the right to complete the pin.

Katate dori Sankyo omote #1

In this *Sankyo uke* attacks with *katate dori (gyaku hanmi)*. You step to the side (*sokumen*) of *uke* to execute the technique. This form of the technique is also a good preparation for *yokomen uchi* attacks.

1) *Uke* attacks with *katate dori*.

2) Step to the side (*sokumen*) and swing your held hand palm up above *uke*'s.

3) Turn your hips, rotate your held hand so that it is palm down and move your arm at shoulder height in front of you releasing *uke*'s grip. Your hands slide to her wrist and elbow.

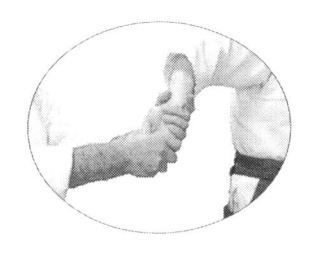

5) Reach under *uke*'s arm and take hold of the side of her hand. Your right hand slides down to capture her fingers and establish the *Sankyo* control.

4) Turn your hips to the right and swing your arms down to break *uke*'s balance.

6) Direct *uke* to the mat and step forward, taking hold of the inside of her elbow with your right hand.

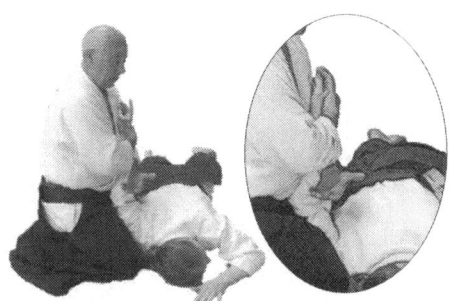

7) Kneel down and apply the *Sankyo* immobilisation, the knife edge of your left hand drawing *uke*'s elbow to your waist.

Sankyo

Katate dori Sankyo ura #1

In this *Sankyo uke* attacks with *katate dori (gyaku hanmi)*. You step to the side (*sokumen*) of *uke* to execute the technique. This form of the technique is also a good preparation for *yokomen uchi* attacks.

1) *Uke* attacks with *katate dori* in *hidari hanmi* (left posture)

2) Step to the side (*sokumen*) and swing your held hand palm up above *uke*'s.

3) Turn your hips, rotate your held hand so that it is palm down and move your arm at shoulder height in front of you releasing *uke*'s grip. Your hands slide to her wrist and elbow.

6) Continuing to pivot on your right foot direct *uke* to the mat.

5) Pivoting on your right foot move your left hand to *uke*'s elbow and pin her arm to her lower back.

4) Step forward on your left leg and reach under her arm with your right hand to establish the *Sankyo* control.

7) Kneel down and control *uke*'s arm, your right hand maintaining the *Sankyo* control and your left hand pinning her shoulder to the mat.

8) Move your left hand to *uke*'s hand, keeping the *Sankyo* control on, and use the knife edge of your right hand to draw her elbow towards your waist. Lift up slightly and turn your shoulders to the right to complete the pin.

Yokomen uchi Sankyo omote

In this *Sankyo uke* attacks with *yokomen uchi*. You step to the side (*sokumen*) of *uke* to intercept the attack and execute the technique.

1) *Uke* attacks with *yokomen uchi*.

2) Step to the side (*sokumen*) as you swing your arm up and to the side' hand palm up, to intercept the attack.

3) Turn your hips, rotate your extended arm so that your hand is palm down and immediately move your arm at shoulder height in front of you.

5) Reach under *uke's* arm and take hold of the side of her hand. Your right hand slides down to capture her fingers and to establish the *Sankyo* control.

4) Holding her arm at wrist and elbow, swing your arms down to break her balance.

6) Direct *uke* to the mat and step forward, taking hold of the inside of her elbow with your right hand.

7) Kneel down and apply the *Sankyo* immobilisation, the knife edge of your left hand drawing *uke's* elbow to your waist.

Yokomen uchi Sankyo ura

In this *Sankyo uke* attacks with *yokomen uchi*. You step to the side (*sokumen*) of *uke* to intercept the attack and execute the technique.

1) *Uke* attacks with *yokomen uchi*.

2) Step to the side (*sokumen*) as you swing your arm up and to the side' hand palm up, to intercept the attack.

3) Turn your hips, rotate your extended arm so that your hand is palm down and immediately move your arm at shoulder height in front of you.

4) Holding her arm at wrist and elbow, step behind *uke* and turn 180°. Swing your arms down to break her balance.

5) Step back on your left leg, reach under *uke's* arm and take hold of the side of her hand. Your left hand slides down to capture her fingers and to establish the *Sankyo* control.

6) Pivoting on your right foot move your left hand to the inside of *uke's* elbow and pin her arm to her lower back.

7) Direct *uke* to the mat.

8) Kneel down and apply the *Sankyo* immobilisation, the knife edge of your right hand drawing *uke's* elbow to your waist.

Katate dori Sankyo omote #2

In this *Sankyo uke* attacks with *katate dori (gyaku hanmi)*. You step to the side and back (*ushiro sokumen*) to execute the technique. This form of the technique is also a good preparation for *chudan tsuki* attacks.

1) *Uke* attacks with *katate dori*.

2) Step back and to the side (*ushiro sokumen*) at the same time taking hold of the back of *uke's* hand with your free hand. *Uke's* weight moves to her front leg.

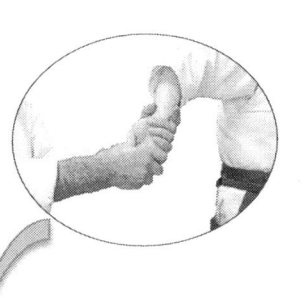

4) Step forward, reach under *uke's* arm and take hold of the side of her hand. Your right hand slides down to capture her fingers and to establish the *Sankyo* control.

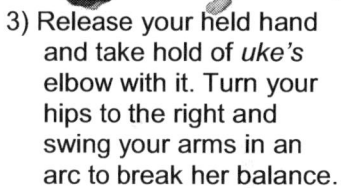

3) Release your held hand and take hold of *uke's* elbow with it. Turn your hips to the right and swing your arms in an arc to break her balance.

5) Direct *uke* to the mat and step forward, taking hold of the inside of her elbow with your right hand.

6) Kneel down and apply the *Sankyo* immobilisation, the knife edge of your left hand drawing *uke's* elbow to your waist.

Katate dori Sankyo ura #2

In this *Sankyo uke* attacks with *katate dori (gyaku hanmi)*. You step to the side (*sokumen*) of *uke* to execute the technique.

1) *Uke* attacks with *katate dori*.

2) Step back and to the side (*ushiro sokumen*) at the same time taking hold of the back of *uke's* hand with your free hand. *Uke's* weight moves to her front leg.

3) Release your held hand. Turn your hips to the left extending *uke* off-balance.

6) Direct *uke* to the mat.

5) Pivoting on your right foot move your left hand to the inside of *uke's* elbow and pin her arm to her lower back.

4) Step behind *uke* and pivot 180° on your right leg. your freed right hand reaches under *uke's* arm and takes hold of the side of her hand. Your left hand slides down to capture her fingers and establish the *Sankyo* control.

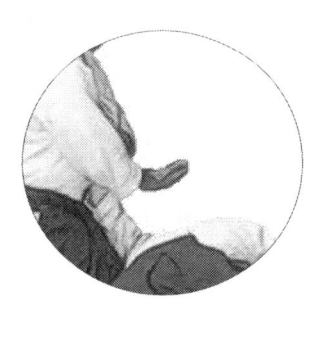

7) Kneel down and apply the *Sankyo* immobilisation, the knife edge of your right hand drawing *uke's* elbow to your waist.

Chudan tsuki Sankyo omote

In this *Sankyo uke* attacks with *chudan tsuki*. You step to the side and back (*ushiro sokumen*) to intercept the attack and execute the technique.

1) *Uke* attacks with *chudan tsuki*.

2) Step back and to the side (*ushiro sokumen*) intercepting and redirecting *uke's* punch. *Uke's* weight moves to her front leg. Your right hand drops onto the back of her hand.

4) Step forward, reach under *uke's* arm and take hold of the side of her hand. Your right hand slides down to capture her fingers and establish the *Sankyo* control.

3) Take hold of *uke's* elbow with your left hand and turn your hips to the right, swinging your arms in an arc to break her balance.

5) Direct *uke* to the mat and step forward, taking hold of the inside of her elbow with your right hand.

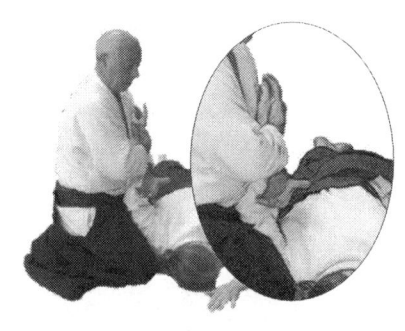

6) Kneel down and apply the *Sankyo* immobilisation, the knife edge of your left hand drawing *uke's* elbow to your waist.

Irimi nage

Simple yet effective, *Irimi nage, or entering throw,* is a favoured technique in multiple attack situations. Your initial entering movement takes you to *uke's* rear blind side and puts you immediately into a strong strategic position. When surrounded by attackers, you can use *Irimi nage* to position yourself outside the attacking perimeter and throw *uke* into the place you formerly occupied.

The table below shows the *Irimi nage* variations described in this section of the book. The *kosa dori* and *katate dori* forms are techniques in themselves but they also serve as preparation for more difficult attacks such as *shomen uchi, yokomen uchi* and *tsuki*.

Attack	*Form*
Kosa dori	*Irimi kaiten*
Shomen uchi	*Irimi kaiten*
Kosa dori	*Irimi tenkan*
Shomen uchi	*Irimi tenkan*
Katate dori	*Sokumen*
Yokomen uchi	*Sokumen*
Katate dori	*Irimi hantenkan*
Yokomen uchi	*Irimi hantenkan*
Katate dori	*Ushiro sokumen*
Chudan tsuki	*Ushiro sokumen*
Kosa dori	*Irimi sokumen*
Chudan tsuki	*Irimi sokumen*
Kosa dori	*Irimi tankan*
Jodan tsuki	*Irimi tenkan*

Kosa dori Irimi nage #1

In this basic *Irimi nage, uke* takes hold of your right wrist. You step forward (*irimi*) to her blind side, turn your hips (*kaiten*) and throw her in the direction that you are facing at the beginning of the technique. This technique is a good preparation for dealing with *shomen uchi, jodan tsuki* and *chudan tsuki* attacks.

1) *Uke* grabs your right wrist with her right hand (*kosa dori*).

2) Step forward (*irimi*) to her right side, place your left hand at the base of her neck and turn to face the same direction.

4) Step forward, throwing her to the mat.

3) Turn your whole body anticlockwise, your upper right arm extending up and forward across her jaw line.

Shomen uchi Irimi nage #1

Uke attacks with *shomen uchi*. You step forward (*irimi*) to her blind side, turn your hips (*kaiten*) and throw her in the direction that you are facing at the beginning of the technique.

1) *Uke* attacks *shomen uchi* and you immediately move forward on your right leg and intercept her right arm with your right arm.

2) Step forward (*irimi*) to her right side, place your left hand at the base of her neck and turn to face the same direction maintaining light contact with her attacking arm.

4) Step forward, throwing her to the mat.

3) Turn your whole body anticlockwise, your upper right arm extending up and forward across her jaw line.

Kosa dori Iriminage #2

In this version of *Irimi nage*, uke takes hold of your right wrist. You step forward to her blind side, draw her off-balance and throw her in the direction of her initial attack. This technique is a good preparation for dealing with *shomen uchi* attacks.

1) *Uke* grabs your left wrist with her left hand (*kosa dori*).

2) Step forward (*irimi*) to her left side, place your right hand at the base of her neck and turn approximately 180° (*kaiten*)

3) Keeping your left arm in front of *uke*, step back on your left leg, drawing her off-balance in front of you.

5)… immediately step forward, throwing her to the mat.

4) As *uke* attempts to regain her balance, you turn your hips to the right and extend your left arm up across her jaw line and …

Irimi nage

Shomen uchi Irimi nage #2

In this *Irimi nage* technique *uke* attacks with *shomen uchi*. You step forward to her blind side, draw her off-balance and throw her.

1) *Uke* attempts a vertical strike to your head *(shomen uchi)*. You immediately intercept her raised arm.

2) Step forward (*irimi*) to her left side, place your right hand at the base of her neck and turn approximately 180° (*kaiten*)

3) Step back on your left leg keeping your left arm in front of her, drawing her off-balance in front of you.

5)... immediately step forward, throwing her to the mat.

4) As *uke* attempts to regain her balance, you turn your hips to the right and extend your left arm up across her jaw line and ...

Katate dori irimi nage #1

1) *Uke* moves towards you and grabs your left wrist with her right hand

2) You step to the side as you swing your left arm palm up to the left.

3) As you extend your arm downwards, breaking her grip, you take hold of her right wrist with your right hand and draw your right foot to the left.

6) Stepping back on your right leg, you draw *uke* off balance in front of you.

5) You then step forward on your left leg and align yourself to her direction.

4) Turning your hips clockwise you reach for the base of her neck.

7) As she attempts to regain her balance, you turn your hips to the left and extend your right arm up across her jaw line.

8) Then you step forward, throwing her to the mat.

Yokomen uchi irimi nage #1

1) *Uke* attacks with *yokomen uchi*.

2) You step to the side as you swing your left arm palm up to the left intercepting the strike.

6) Stepping back on your right leg, you draw *uke* off balance in front of you.

5) You then step forward on your left leg and align yourself to her direction.

7) As she attempts to regain her balance, you turn your hips to the left and extend your right arm up across her jaw line.

8) Then you step forward, throwing her to the mat.

Katate dori irimi nage #2

In this *katate dori* form of *Irimi nage,* you move in front of *uke* and then execute the technique. This form of the technique is a good preparation for dealing with a *yokomen uchi* attack.

1) *Uke* attacks with *katate dori*.

2) You step diagonally forward as you swing your left arm palm up to the left drawing her slightly off-balance.

3) As you extend your arm downwards, draw your left foot behind the right foot.

4) Turn your hips clockwise and take hold of *uke*'s right wrist with your right hand.

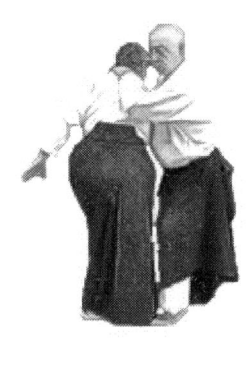

5) Reach for the base of her neck you then step forward on your left leg.

6) Turning clockwise and stepping back on your right leg, you draw *uke* off balance in front of you.

7) As she attempts to regain her balance, you turn your hips to the left and extend your right arm up across her jaw line.

8) Then you step forward, throwing her to the mat.

Yokomen uchi Irimi nage #2

In this *Irimi nage*, uke attacks *yokomen uchi*. Intercepting the attack you move diagonally forward and perform the technique.

1) *Uke* attacks with *yokomen uchi*

2) You step diagonally forward as you swing your left arm palm up to intercept her strike.

3) As you extend your arm downwards, draw your left foot behind the right foot.

4) Turn your hips clockwise and take hold of *uke*'s right wrist with your right hand.

5) Reach for the base of her neck you then step forward on your left leg.

6) Turning clockwise and stepping back on your right leg, you draw *uke* off balance in front of you.

7) As she attempts to regain her balance, you turn your hips to the left and extend your right arm up across her jaw line.

8) Then you step forward, throwing her to the mat.

Katate dori Irimi nage #3

In this version of *Irimi nage, uke* grabs your left wrist with her right hand moving towards you. You step diagonally to your rear, drawing her weight to her front leg, and throw her in the direction that she was facing at the beginning of the technique.

1) *Uke* attacks with *katate dori*.

2) You immediately step diagonally to your rear drawing her weight on to her front leg.

3) You take hold of her left wrist with your right hand, disengaging your held left wrist.

6) … step back drawing her off balance in front of you.

5) Turn to face the same direction as *uke* and …

4) Reaching for the base of her neck you then step forward on your left leg.

7) Turn your hips anticlockwise, your upper right arm extending up and forward across her jaw line.

8) Step forward, throwing her to the mat.

Chudan tsuki Iriminage #1

In this version of *Irimi nage*, uke attacks with *chudan tsuki*. You step diagonally to your rear, intercept her attacking arm, draw her weight to her front leg, and throw her in the direction that she was facing at the beginning of the technique.

1) *Uke* attacks *chudan tsuki*.

2) You immediately step diagonally to your rear intercepting her attacking arm.

3) You take hold of her left wrist with your right hand as you draw your right foot off the line of attack.

6) ... step back drawing her off balance in front of you.

5) Turn to face the same direction as *uke* and

4) Reaching for the base of her neck you then step forward on your left leg.

7) Turn your hips anticlockwise, your upper right arm extending up and forward across her jaw line.

8) Step forward, throwing her to the mat.

Kosa dori Irimi nage #3

In this version of *Irimi nage, uke* grabs your left wrist with her right hand moving towards you. You step diagonally to your rear, drawing her weight to her front leg, and throw her in the direction that she was facing at the beginning of the technique. This variation is a good preparation for *chudan tsuki irimi nage*.

1) *Uke* attacks *kosa dori*.

2) You immediately step diagonally forward to your left drawing her weight on to her front leg.

3) As your right arm begins to swing up you draw your right foot to the left.

4) Reaching for the base of her neck you then step forward on your left leg. and turn to face the same direction as *uke*.

5) Step back drawing her off balance in front of you.

6) Turn your hips anticlockwise, your upper right arm extending up and forward across her jaw line.

7) Step forward, throwing her to the mat.

Chudan tsuki Irimi nage #2

In this version of *Irimi nage, uke* attacks *chudan tsuki*. You step diagonally forward, leading her weight to her front leg, and throw her in the direction that she was facing at the beginning of the technique.

1) *Uke* attacks *chudan tsuki*

2) You immediately step diagonally forward to your left leading her weight on to her front leg.

3) As your right arm begins to swing up you draw your right foot to the left.

6) Turn your hips anticlockwise, your upper right arm extending up and forward across her jaw line.

5) Step back drawing her off balance in front of you.

4) Reaching for the base of her neck you then step forward on your left leg. and turn to face the same direction as *uke*.direction as *uke*.

7) Step forward, throwing her to the mat.

Kosa dori Irimi nage #4

In this version of *Irimi nage, uke* attempts to grab your wrist. You swing your grasped arm up, step deeply to her blind side and complete the technique. This form is a good preparation for *jodan tsuki* attacks.

1) *Uke* attacks *kosa dori*.

2) You immediately swing your arm up and...

3) ... step deeply to her blind side, reaching for the base of her neck with your free hand.

6) Turn your hips clockwise, your upper left arm extending up and forward across her jaw line.

5) Step back drawing her off balance in front of you.

4) Align yourself in the same direction as *uke*.

7) Step forward, throwing her to the mat.

Jodan tsuki Irimi nage

In this version of *Irimi nage*, uke strikes *jodan tsuki*. You intercept her attack, step deeply to her blind side and complete the technique.

1) *Uke* attacks *jodan tsuki*.

2) You immediately swing your arm up to intercept the punch and...

3) ... step deeply to her blind side, reaching for the base of her neck with your free hand.

6) Turn your hips clockwise, your upper left arm extending up and forward across her jaw line.

5) Step back drawing her off balance in front of you.

4) Align yourself in the same direction as *uke*.

7) Step forward, throwing her to the mat.

Irimi nage

Shiho nage

Shiho nage (four-direction throw) allows you to take firm control of *uke's* attacking arm and use it to project or pin him in any direction. The technique requires you to turn your hips so that *uke's* arm is aligned with yours and then lift your arms and his arm to head height before passing under his arm. This can a very dangerous technique and must be practised with care for *uke's* safety. Allow *uke's* arm to bend fully at the elbow before throwing him, otherwise an injury may result.

The examples show the *omote* (*irimi*) version but only a relatively small adjustment is required to vary the direction of the throw or immobilisation.

The table below shows the *shiho nage* variations described in this section of the book. The *kosa dori* and *katate dori* forms are techniques in themselves but they also serve as preparation for more difficult attacks such as *shomen uchi, yokomen uchi* and *tsuki*.

Attack	*Form*
Kosa dori	*Yoko ashi*
Shomen uchi	*Yoko ashi*
Jodan tsuki	*Yoko ashi*
Katate dori	*Sokumen*
Yokomen uchi	*Sokumen*
Katate dori	*Irimi hantenkan*
Yokomen uchi	*Irimi hantenkan*
Katate dori	*Ushiro sokumen*
Chudan tsuki	*Ushiro sokumen*

Kosa dori Shiho nage #1

In this *Shiho nage uke* attacks with *kosa dori (ai-hanmi katate dori)*. You step to the side (*yoko ashi*) and then execute the technique. This form of *shiho nage* is also a preparation for *shomen uchi* and *jodan tsuki* attacks.

1) *Uke* attacks with *kosa dori*.

2) You step to the side as you swing your right hand up to about head height.

3) Your left arm swings up to disengage *uke's* hand.

6) Turn your hips to the right keeping your hands in front of you so that *uke's* elbow is drawn towards yours.

5) Grasp his wrist with your right hand and the thumb side of his hand with your left hand.

4) Swing both of your hands down to waist height.

7) Swing your arms up to head height, step forward on your left leg and turn 180°.

8) Bend your front knee and swing your arms down.

9) Pin *uke* or project him downwards.

Shomen uchi Shiho nage

In this *Shiho nage uke* attacks with *shomen uchi*. You step to the side (*yoko ashi*) intercept and deflect his attack, and then execute the technique.

1) *Uke* attacks with *shomen uchi*.

2) You step to the side as you swing your right hand up to about head height intercepting the attack.

3) Your left arm swings up to engage *uke's* hand.

6) Turn your hips to the right keeping your hands in front of you so that *uke's* elbow touches yours.

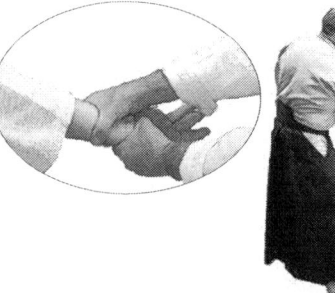

5) Grasp his wrist with your right hand and the thumb side of his hand with your left hand.

4) Swing both of your hands down to waist height.

7) Swing your arms up to head height, step forward on your left leg and turn 180°.

8) Bend your front knee and swing your arms down.

9) Pin *uke* or project him downwards.

Jodan tsuki Shiho nage

In this *Shiho nage uke* attacks with *jodan tsuki,* a straight punch to your head. You step to the side (*yoko ashi*) intercept and deflect his attack, and then execute the technique.

1) *Uke* attacks with *jodan tsuki*.

2) You step to the side as you swing your right hand up to about head height intercepting the attack.

3) Your left arm immediately swings up to deflect *uke's* hand.

5) Turn your hips to the right keeping your hands in front of you so that *uke's* elbow touches yours.

4) Swing both of your hands down to waist height and grasp his wrist with your right hand and the thumb side of his hand with your left hand.

6) Swing your arms up to head height, step forward on your left leg and turn 180°.

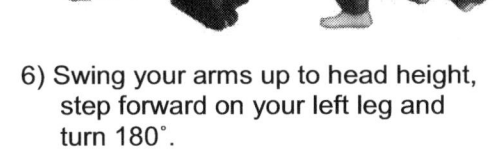

7) Bend your front knee and swing your arms down.

8) Pin *uke* or project him downwards.

Katate dori Shiho nage #1

In this *Shiho nage uke* attacks with *katate dori*. You step to the side (*sokumen*) and then execute the technique. This form of *shiho nage* is also a preparation for *yokomen uchi* attacks.

1) *Uke* attacks with *katate dori*.

2) You step to the side (*sokumen*) as you swing your left arm to the left so that your hand, palm up is above *uke's*. You take hold of his wrist with your right hand.

4) Turn your hips keeping your hands in front of you so that *uke's* elbow touches yours.

3) Disengage your left hand from his grip and take hold of his hand with it.

5) Swing your arms up to head height, step forward on your left leg and turn 180°.

6) Bend your front knee and swing your arms down, pinning *uke* or projecting him downwards.

Yokomen uchi Shiho nage #1

In this *Shiho nage uke* attacks with *yokomen uchi*. You step to the side (*sokumen*), intercepting his attack from above with a straight arm, hand palm up, and then execute the technique.

1) *Uke* attacks with *yokomen uchi*.

2) You step to the side (*sokumen*) as you swing your left arm to the left so that your hand, palm up is above *uke's*, intercepting his strike. You swing your left arm down and take hold of his wrist with your right hand.

4) Turn your hips keeping your hands in front of you so that *uke's* elbow touches yours.

3) Take hold of the thumb side of his hand with your left hand.

5) Swing your arms up to head height, step forward on your left leg and turn 180°.

6) Bend your front knee and swing your arms down, pinning *uke* or projecting him downwards.

Katate dori Shiho nage #2

In this *Shiho nage uke* attacks with *katate dori*. You step in front (*irimi hantenkan*) and then execute the technique.

1) *Uke* attacks with *katate dori*.

2) You step diagonally forward on your right leg and make a small adjustment with your left leg as you swing your left arm to the left so that your hand, palm up, is above *uke's*. You take hold of his wrist with your right hand.

4) Turn your hips keeping your hands in front of you so that *uke's* elbow touches yours.

3) Disengage your left hand from his grip and take hold of his hand with it.

5) Swing your arms up to head height, step forward on your left leg and turn 180°.

6) Bend your front knee and swing your arms down, pinning *uke* or projecting him downwards.

Yokomen uchi Shiho nage #2

In this *Shiho nage uke* attacks with *yokomen uchi*. Intercepting his attack, you step in front (*irimi hantenkan*) and then execute the technique.

1) *Uke* attacks with *yokomen uchi*.

2) You step diagonally forward in front of *uke* on your right leg and make a small adjustment with your left leg as you swing your left arm to the left so that your hand, palm up, intercepts *uke's* attack.

3) You guide his arm down and grasp his wrist with your right hand.

5) Swing your arms up to head height, step forward on your left leg and turn 180°.

4) Turn your hips keeping your hands in front of you so that *uke's* elbow touches yours.

6) Bend your front knee and swing your arms down, pinning *uke* or projecting him downwards.

Katate dori Shiho nage #3

In this *Shiho nage uke* attacks with *katate dori*. You step to the side and your rear (*ushiro sokumen*) and then execute the technique. This form of *shiho nage* is also a preparation for *chudan tsuki* attacks and straight thrusts with a knife.

1) *Uke* attacks with *katate dori*.

2) You step to the side and rear drawing *uke*'s weight on to his front leg. You take hold of his wrist with your right and release your left hand from his grip.

4) Turn your hips keeping your hands in front of you so that *uke*'s elbow touches yours.

3) Take hold of the thumb side of his hand with your left hand.

5) Swing your arms up to head height, step forward on your left leg and turn 180°.

6) Bend your front knee and swing your arms down, pinning *uke* or projecting him downwards.

Chudan tsuki Shiho nage

In this *Shiho nage uke* attacks with *chudan tsuki*. You step to the side and your rear (*ushiro sokumen*) and then execute the technique.

1) *Uke* attacks with *chudan tsuki*.

2) You step back and to your left while intercepting *uke's* straight thrust to your mid-section. You immediately take hold of his wrist with your right hand.

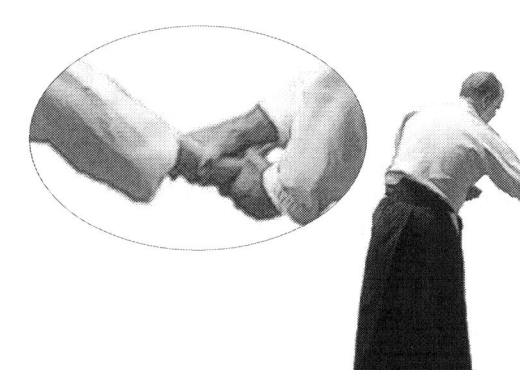

3) Take hold of the thumb side of his hand with your left hand.

4) Turn your hips keeping your hands in front of you so that *uke's* elbow touches yours.

5) Swing your arms up to head height, step forward on your left leg and turn 180°.

6) Bend your front knee and swing your arms down, pinning *uke* or projecting him downwards.

Kote gaeshi

Kote gaeshi, small hand-turn, is classed as *tekubi waza*, that is a hand technique. It is a very effective form of control that can be used to project or immobilise *uke*. The wrist, elbow and shoulder joints are all put under stress during the execution of this technique, so *tori* must apply it carefully. When the technique is applied at speed with full commitment, *uke* must perform a flip and land on her back to avoid arm damage. When the technique is applied slowly and carefully, *uke* has time to roll backwards safely.

The table below shows the *Kote gaeshi* variations described in this section of the book. The *kosa dori* and *katate dori* forms are techniques in themselves but they also serve as preparation for more difficult attacks such as *shomen uchi, yokomen uchi* and *tsuki*.

Attack	*Form*
Kosa dori	*Yoko ashi*
Shomen uchi	*Yoko ashi*
Jodan tsuki	*Yoko ashi*
Katate dori	*Sokumen*
Yokomen uchi	*Sokumen*
Katate dori	*Irimi hantenkan*
Yokomen uchi	*Irimi hantenkan*
Kosa dori	*Irimi sokumen*
Chudan tsuki	*Irimi sokumen*

Kosa dori Kote gaeshi #1

In this version of *Kote gaeshi* you move to your right in front of *uke*, swing up your held arm, break her grip and establish the wrist control which you then use to throw her down. This form of the technique can also be used as a preparation for *shomen uchi* and *jodan tsuki* attacks.

1) *Uke* attacks with *kosa dori*.

2) Move to your right and extend your right arm upwards with your left hand contacting *uke's* wrist. Break her grip and maintain control of her wrist with your right hand.

3) Step to *uke's* side and turn about 180° *(irimi tenkan)* as your left hand grasps her wrist from above.

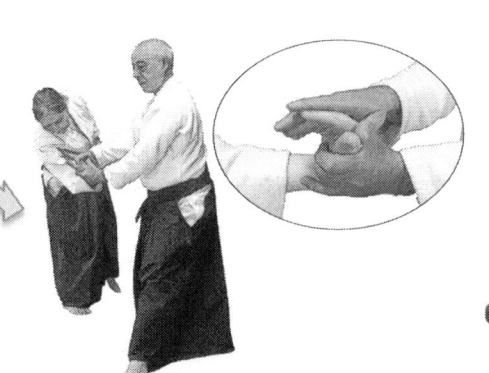

4) Leaving your left arm extended step back on your left leg and begin to turn *uke's* hand outwards.

5) fold your right hand over *uke's* hand and rotate your hips left.

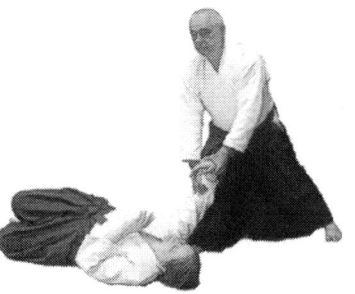

6) Follow as *uke* falls to the mat and take hold of her elbow.

7) Move around uke's head, turn her onto her front and pin her arm.

Shomen uchi Kote gaeshi

In this version of *Kote gaeshi* you move to your right in front of *uke*, intercept her vertical strike and establish the wrist control which you then use to throw her down.

1) *Uke* attacks with *shomen uchi*.

2) Move to your right in front of *uke* and extend your right arm upwards, intercepting her attack, and guide her arm down. Maintain control of her arm with your right hand.

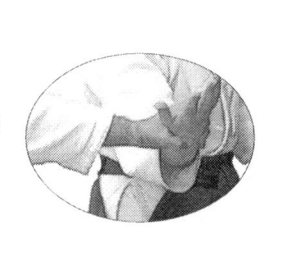

4) Leaving your left arm extended step back on your left leg and begin to turn *uke's* hand outwards.

3) Step to *uke's* side and turn about 180° *(irimi tenkan)* as your left hand grasps her wrist from above.

5) Fold your right hand over *uke's* hand and rotate your hips left.

6) Follow as *uke* falls to the mat and take hold of her elbow.

7) Move around *uke's* head, turning her onto her front and then pin her arm.

Jodan tsuki Kote gaeshi

In this version of *Kote gaeshi* you move to your right in front of *uke*, intercept her punch to your face and establish the wrist control which you then use to throw her down.

1) *Uke* attacks with *jodan tsuki*.

2) Move to your right in front of *uke* and extend your right arm upwards, intercepting her attack, and guide her arm down. Maintain control of her arm with your right hand.

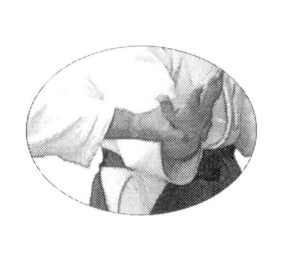

4) Leaving your left arm extended step back on your left leg and begin to turn *uke's* hand outwards.

3) Step to *uke's* side and turn about 180° *(irimi tenkan)* as your left hand grasps her wrist from above.

5) Fold your right hand over *uke's* hand and rotate your hips left.

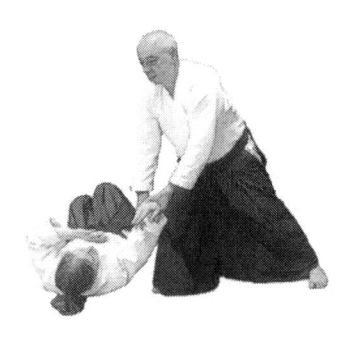

6) Follow as *uke* falls to the mat and take hold of her elbow.

7) Move around *uke's* head, turning her onto her front and then pin her arm.

Katate dori Kote gaeshi #1

In this version of *Kote gaeshi* you move to *uke's side* using a *sokumen* movement, swing up your held arm, break her grip and establish the wrist control which you then use to throw her down. This form of the technique can also be used as a preparation for *yokomen uchi* attacks.

1) *Uke* attacks with *katate dori*.

2) Move to your left to *uke's* side (*sokumen*) extending your held arm out to the side palm up releasing her grip on your wrist. Take hold from underneath with your right hand.

4) Leaving your left arm extended step back on your left leg and begin to turn *uke's* hand outwards.

3) As you step forward and turn (*irimi tenkan*) you replace your right hand grip with your left hand from above, establishing the *Kote gaeshi* control.

5) Fold your right hand over *uke's* hand and rotate your hips left.

6) Follow as *uke* falls to the mat and take hold of her elbow.

7) Move around *uke's* head, turning her onto her front and then pin her arm.

Kote gaeshi

Yokomen uchi Kote gaeshi #1

In this version of *Kote gaeshi* you move to your left, swing up your left arm to intercept her strike and establish the wrist control which you then use to throw her down.

1) *Uke* attacks with *yokomen uchi*.

2) Move to your left to *uke's* side (*sokumen*) extending your left arm out to the side palm up intercepting her attack. Direct her wrist towards your right hand.

3) As you step forward and turn (*irimi tenkan*) you replace your right hand grip with your left hand from above, establishing the *Kote gaeshi* control.

4) Leaving your left arm extended step back on your left leg and begin to turn *uke's* hand outwards.

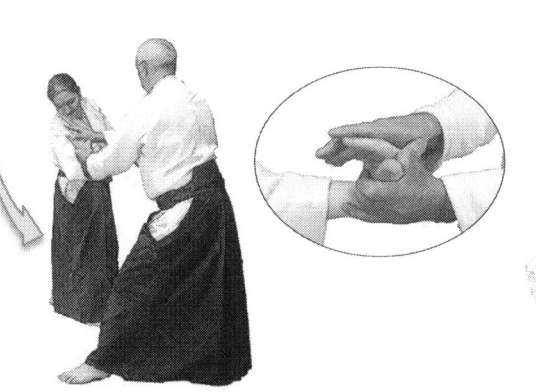

5) Fold your right hand over *uke's* hand and rotate your hips left.

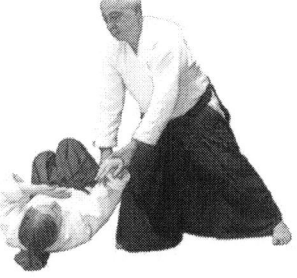

6) Follow as *uke* falls to the mat and take hold of her elbow.

7) Move around *uke's* head, turning her onto her front and then pin her arm.

Katate dori Kote gaeshi #2

In this version of *Kote gaeshi* you move in front of *uke* using an *irimi hantenkan* movement, swing up your held arm, break her grip and establish the wrist control which you then use to throw her down. This form of the technique can also be used as a preparation for *yokomen uchi* attacks.

1) *Uke* attacks with *katate dori*.

2) Move to your right (*irimi hantenkan*) extending your held arm out to the side palm up releasing her grip on your wrist. Take hold from underneath with your right hand.

4) Leaving your left arm extended step back on your left leg and begin to turn *uke's* hand outwards.

3) As you step forward and turn (*irimi tenkan*) you replace your right hand grip with your left hand from above, establishing the *Kote gaeshi* control.

5) Fold your right hand over *uke's* hand and rotate your hips left.

6) Step forward as *uke* falls to the mat and take hold of her elbow.

7) Move around *uke's* head, turning her onto her front and then pin her arm.

Yokomen uchi Kote gaeshi #2

In this version of *Kote gaeshi* you move to your right in front of *uke*, intercepting her attack, and establishing the wrist control which you then use to throw her down.

1) *Uke* attacks with *yokomen uchi*.

2) Move to your right (*irimi hantenkan*) extending your left arm out to the side palm up intercepting her attack. Take hold from underneath with your right hand.

4) Leaving your left arm extended step back on your left leg and begin to turn *uke's* hand outwards.

3) As you step forward and turn (*irimi tenkan*) you replace your right hand grip with your left hand from above, establishing the *Kote gaeshi* control.

5) Fold your right hand over *uke's* hand and rotate your hips left. Follow as *uke* falls to the mat and take hold of her elbow.

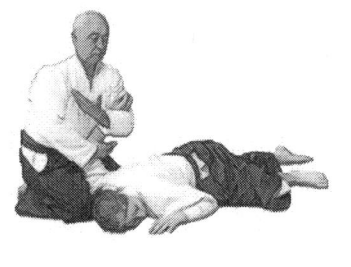

6) Move around *uke's* head, turning her onto her front and then pin her arm.

Kosa dori Kote gaeshi #2

In this version of *Kote gaeshi* you move diagonally forward to *uke's* side, drawing her off balance prior to establishing the *Kote gaeshi* control and throwing her down to the mat. This form of the technique can also be used as a preparation for *chudan tsuki* attacks.

1) *Uke* attacks with *kosa dori*.

2) Turn your hips and lead *uke* past you. Your arm swings over hers and breaks her grip.

4) Leaving your left arm extended step back on your left leg and begin to turn *uke's* hand outwards.

3) Step to *uke's* side and turn about 180° *(irimi tenkan)* as your left hand grasps her wrist from above.

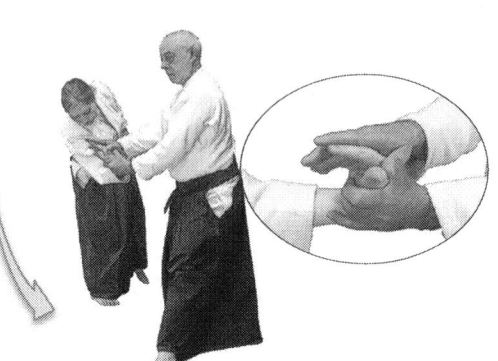

5) fold your right hand over *uke's* hand and rotate your hips left.

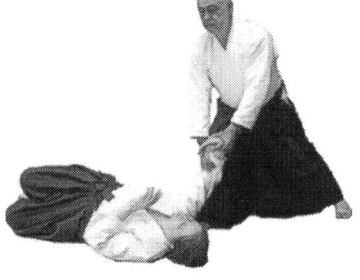

6) Follow as *uke* falls to the mat and take hold of her elbow.

7) Move around *uke's* head, turn her onto her front and pin her arm.

Chudan tsuki Kote gaeshi

In this version of *Kote gaeshi* you move diagonally forward to *uke's* side, intercepting her punch and drawing her off balance prior to establishing the *Kote gaeshi* control and throwing her down to the mat.

1) *Uke* attacks with *chudan tsuki*.

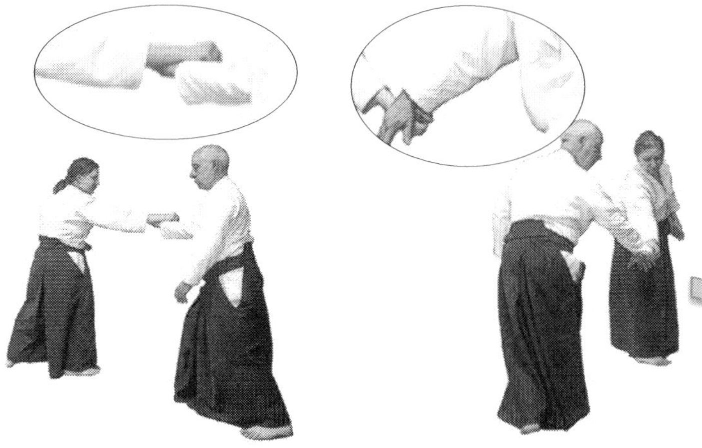

2) Turn your hips and lead *uke* past you. Your arm makes contact from underneath and then rotates around her wrist to the outside of her arm.

3) Step to *uke's* side and turn about 180° *(irimi tenkan)* as your left hand grasps her wrist from above.

4) Leaving your left arm extended step back on your left leg and begin to turn *uke's* hand outwards.

5) Fold your right hand over *uke's* hand and rotate your hips left.

6) Follow as *uke* falls to the mat and take hold of her elbow.

7) Move around *uke's* head, turn her onto her front and pin her arm.

Kokyu nage

Kokyu nage can be roughly translated as "breath throw" or "timing throw" and the term covers many different types of *Aikido* techniques, some basic and others advanced. The variations described in this section are some of the more basic forms.

Kokyu nage techniques, although many and varied, all utilise the same small set of basic principles, namely

- Moving off the line of attack and blending with it.
- Precise timing.
- Redirecting the attacking energy to unsettle *uke*'s balance.
- Using whole body movement to project *uke* away.

The table below shows the *Kokyu nage* variations described in this section of the book. The *kosa dori* and *katate dori* forms are techniques in themselves but they also serve as preparation for more difficult attacks such as *shomen uchi, yokomen uchi* and *tsuki*.

Attack	*Form*
Kosa dori	Yoko ashi
Shomen uchi	Yoko ashi
Katate dori	Sokumen
Yokomen uchi	Sokumen
Katate dori	Irimi hantenkan
Yokomen uchi	Irimi hantenkan
Jodan tsuki	Yoko ashi
Katate dori	Ushiro sokumen
Chudan tsuki	Ushiro sokumen

Kosa dori Kokyu nage #1

In this basic *Kokyu nage* you move to your right in front of *uke*, swing up your held arm to unbalance him before throwing him backwards.

1) *Uke* attacks with *kosa dori*.

2) Move to your right and extend your right arm upwards, drawing *uke* off-balance.

4) As *uke* attempts to regain his balance you extend your left arm across his shoulder line step behind him with your left leg and turn your hips to the left as you extend out and down with both arms.

3) Swing your arm down as you turn your hips to the right.

Shomen uchi Kokyu nage

In this basic *Kokyu nage* you move to your right in front of *uke*, intercepting his attack and then throwing him backwards.

1) *Uke* attacks with *shomen uchi*.

2) Move to your right intercepting *uke's* attack with your right hand immediately followed by your left hand which cuts his arm downwards.

4) As *uke* attempts to regain his balance you extend your left arm across his shoulder line step behind him with your left leg and turn your hips to the left as you extend out and down with both arms.

3) Grasp his wrist with your right hand, turn to your right and lead *uke* off-balance.

Jodan tsuki Kokyu nage

In this basic *Kokyu nage* you move to your right *(yoko ashi)* in front of uke, intercepting his attack and then throwing him backwards.

1) *Uke* attacks with *jodan tsuki*.

2) Move to your right intercepting *uke's* attack with your right hand.

4) As *uke* attempts to regain his balance you extend your left arm across his shoulder line step behind him with your left leg and turn your hips to the left as you extend out and down with both arms.

3) Swing your right arm down and turn your hips to the right, unbalancing *uke*.

Katate dori Kokyu nage #1

In this basic *Kokyu nage* you move to the side of *uke*, unbalancing him and then throwing him backwards. This variation can be used as a preparation for a *yokomen uchi* attack.

1) *Uke* attacks with *katate dori*. Step to your left (*sokumen*) swinging your arm palm up above *uke's* hand and breaking his grip.

2) Extend your left arm high across *uke's* chest and your right arm in front of you, over his right arm.

4) Turn your hips to the left as you continue to extend out and down with both arms.

3) Open your shoulder joints and extend both arms outwards as you step behind uke on your left leg.

Yokomen uchi Kokyu nage #1

In this basic *Kokyu nage* you move to the side of *uke*, intercepting his attack him and then throwing him backwards.

1) *Uke* attacks with *yokomen uchi*. Step to your left (*sokumen*) swinging your arm palm up above *uke's* hand, intercepting his attack.

2) Draw his arm down and grasp his wrist with your right hand.

4) Turn your hips to the left as you continue to extend out and down with both arms.

3) Open your shoulder joint and extend your left arm outwards as you step behind *uke* on your left leg.

Katate dori Kokyu nage #2

In this basic *Kokyu nage* you move in front of *uke (irimi hantenkan)*, unbalancing him and then throwing him backwards. This variation can be used as a preparation for a *yokomen uchi* attack.

1) *Uke* attacks with *katate dori*. Step to your right (*irimi*) swinging your arm palm up above *uke's* hand and breaking his grip. Adjust the position of your left leg (*hantenkan*). And grasp his right wrist with your right hand.

3) Extend your left arm across *uke's* upper body as you step deeply to his rear.

2) Turn your hips to the right, drawing *uke* off-balance.

Yokomen uchi Kokyu nage #2

In this basic *Kokyu nage* you move in front of *uke (irimi hantenkan)*, intercepting his *yokomen uchi* attack, and then throwing him backwards.

1) *Uke* attacks with *yokomen uchi*. Step to your right (*irimi*) swinging your arm palm up above *uke's* hand intercepting his strike. Adjust the position of your left leg (*hantenkan*) and draw his arm down to waist height.

3) Extend your left arm across *uke's* upper body as you step deeply to his rear and project him to the mat.

2) Grasp *uke's* right wrist with your right hand and turn your hips to the right, drawing him off-balance.

Katate dori Kokyu nage #3

In this *Kokyu nage* you move to your rear drawing *uke* foward. This variation can be used as a preparation for a *chudan tsuki* attack.

1) *Uke* attacks with *katate dori*. Step diagonally back on your left leg (*ushiro sokumen*) drawing *uke's* weight towards his front leg.

3) Step behind *uke* swing your left arm forward and up across his upper body, your right arm following.

2) Turn the palm of your left hand up and turn your hips to the right, unbalancing *uke* and breaking his grip.

Chudan tsuki Kokyu nage #1

In this *Kokyu nage* you move diagonally to your rear while intercepting *uke's* attack.

1) *Uke* attacks with *chudan tsuki*. Step diagonally back on your left leg (*ushiro sokumen*), moving out of range and intercepting *uke's* right arm with your left hand.

3) Step behind *uke* swing your left arm forward and up across his upper body, your right arm following.

2) Turn the palm of your left hand up and turn your hips to the right.

Glossary

The meaning of Japanese terms used in the text, with an approximate guide to pronunciation.

Term	Pronunciation	Meaning
Ai-hanmi	Eye han-mee	Partners facing each other in the same posture
Aikido	Eye-kee-dough	Harmony ki way
Atemi	A-temmee	Strike
Bokken	Bocken	Wooden sword
Chudan tsuki	Choo-dan tskee	Punch to mid –section
Dojo	Dough-joe	Practice room
Domo arigato gozai mashita	Dough-mow-arrigattoe-goes-eye-mashta	Thank you (very formal)
Furitama	Fooree tamma	Shaking exercise
Gedan tsuki	Geddan tskee	Punch to below waist
Gyaku-hanmi	Gee-a-koo han-mee	Partners facing each other in opposite postures
Han tenkan	Han-tenkan	Half turn
Hara	Harra	Centre, located just below navel
Hidari-hanmi	Hiddarree han-mee	Left posture
Ikkyo	Ikkyoe	First form
Irimi ashi	Irrimmee ashy	Entering step
Irimi sokumen	Irrimmee sokoomen	Step forward and turn
Irimi tenkan	Irrimmee tenkan	Step forward with full turn turn
Irimi nage	Irrimmee naggay	Entering throw
Jo	Joe	Wooden staff
Jodan tsuki	Joe-dan tskee	Punch to head
Junbi taiso	Junbee tie-sew	Body exercises
Kaiten	Kie-ten	Turn
Kamiza	Kammee-zah	Place in dojo where photograph of the Founder is positioned. Also known as *Shomen*

Glossary

Kata dori	*Katta dorry*	Shoulder grab
Kata dori jodan tsuki	*Katta dorry joe-dan tskee*	Shoulder grab and straight head punch
Kata dori shomen uchi	*Katta dorry show-men oochee*	Shoulder grab and vertical head strike
Kata dori yokomen uchi	*Katta dorry yoe-koe-men oochee*	Shoulder grab and side strike to head
Katate dori	*Ka-ta-tay dorry*	Wrist grab
Keikogi	*Kay-koe-gee*	Training uniform
Ki	*Kee*	Life force
Kokyu	*Koe-kyoo*	Breath
Kokyu nage	*Koe-kyoo naggay*	Breath/timing throw
Kosa dori	*Koe-za dorry*	Wrist grab also known as ai-hanmi katate dori
Kote gaeshi	*Koe-tay-gie-shee*	Small hand-turn
Mai ukemi	*My-oo-kemmee*	Forward breakfall
Migi-hanmi	*Miggee han-mee*	Right posture
Morote dori	*Morrow-tay dorry*	Two hands grab arm
Mune dori	*Moonay dorry*	Grab to middle of chest
Nikyo	*Nikyoe*	Second form
Obi	*Owe-bee*	Belt
Okuri ashi	*Oh-koory ashy*	Move forward starting with front leg
Omote	*Oh-moe-tay*	Enter in front
Onegaeshimasu	*Onny gaishi mass*	Please, let's practice
Rei	*Ray*	Formal bow
Ryokata dori	*Ry-oh katta dorry*	Both shoulders grabbed
Ryote dori	*Ry-oh tay dorry*	Both wrists grabbed
Sankyo	*Sankyoe*	Third form
Seiza	*Say-za*	Sitting posture
Sensei	*Sen-say*	Teacher
Shiho nage	*Shee-hoe naggay*	Four-direction throw
Shikko	*Shi-koe*	Knee walking
Shomen uchi	*Show-men oochee*	Top head strike

Glossary

Sokumen	*Sokoomen*	Step to the side and turn
Tai sabaki	*Tie sabbakee*	Body movements
Tanto	*Tan-toe*	Wooden knife
Tekubi waza	*Te-koobee wazza*	Hand/wrist techniques
Tenkan	*Tenkan*	Full turn pivoting on front foot
Tori	*Torry*	Defender/performer of technique
Tori fune	*Torry foon-ay*	Rowing exercise
Tsugi ashi	*Tsoo-gee ashy*	Move forward starting with rear leg
Uchi	*Oo-chee*	Strike
<u>**Uke**</u>	*Oo-kay*	Attacker/Receiver
Ukemi	*Oo-kemmee*	*Uke* receiving technique
Ura	*Oo-ra*	Enter to the rear
Ushiro ashi	*Oo-shee-roe ashy*	Back step
Ushiro eri dori	*Oosheeroe erry dorry*	Grab collar from rear
Ushiro katate dori kubishime	*Oosheeroe ka-ta-tay dorry*	Rear choke and wrist grab
Ushiro mune dakeshime	*Oosheeroe moonay dakka-shimmay*	Bear hug from the rear
Ushiro ryokata dori	*Oosheeroe rie-oh katta dorry*	Both shoulders grabbed from rear
Ushiro ryote dori	*Oosheeroe rie-oh-tay dorry*	Both wrists grabbed from rear
Ushiro sokumen	*Oo-shee-roe sokoomen*	Step back and turn
Ushiro ukemi	*Oo-shee-roe oo-kemmee*	Backward breakfall
Yoko ashi	*Yoe-koe ashy*	Side step
Yokomen uchi	*Yoe-koe-men oochee*	Side head strike
Zori	*Zorree*	Sandals

Printed in Great Britain
by Amazon